TEMPERA MYSTICISM

SHIRLEY ANN MILLER

Tempera Mysticism

SHIRLEY ANN MILLER

STARBURST PUBLISHERS

P.O. Box 4123, Lancaster, Pennsylvania 17604

To schedule Author appearances write:
Author Appearances, Starburst Promotions, P. O. Box 4123, Lancaster, PA 17604 or call (717) 293-0939.

Credits:

Unless otherwise noted, all Scripture quotations are from the King James Version or the New International Version.

Cover art by Dave Ivey

We, the Publisher and Author, declare that to the best of our knowledge all material (quoted or not) contained herein is accurate; and we shall not be held liable for the same.

TEMPERAMYSTICISM
Copyright © 1991 by Shirley Ann Miller
All rights reserved.

This book may not be used or reproduced in any manner, in whole or in part, stored in a retrieval system or transmitted in any form by any means, electronic, mechanical, photocopy, recording, or otherwise, without written permission of the publisher, except as provided by USA copyright law.

First Printing, June 1991

ISBN: 0-914984-30-6
Library of Congress Catalog Number 91-065106

Printed in the United States of America

Acknowledgements

Thank you

to my Lord and Savior Jesus Christ,
the Author and Finisher of our faith;

My family and friends for their love,
prayers, encouragement, and patience:

Jennifer
Douglas
Gregory
Sarah
Jim
Marie
Paul
Gary
Nellie
Muriel
Linda
Gail
Betty

and the members of the
Dayton Christian Scribes.

Contents

	Introduction	11
1.	**The Temperaments**	21
2.	**The New Age Movement, Christians, and the Temperaments**	37
3.	**Where did the Temperaments Originate?**	45
4.	**The Development of the Four Temperaments**	55
5.	**The Ancient Philosopher's Religion**	69
6.	**Astrology Among the Graeco-Roman Civilizations**	77
7.	**The Temperaments, Astrology, and Medicine**	87
8.	**The Philosophy of the Soul**	95
9.	**Temperaments or TemperaMysticsm**	101
10.	**The Enneagram, Astrology, and the Temperaments**	119
11.	**Conclusion**	135
	Historical References of the Temperaments	151
	Reference Bibliography	159
	General Bibliography	165

Biography

Shirley Ann Miller was a professional astrologer deeply involved in the world of the occult. For over 12 years she spent many hours counseling numerous clients, interpreting horoscopes, and forecasting future events. Her prognostications gained her a reputation and notoriety which brought television and radio appearances, newspaper articles, and speaking engagements.

After many years of professional success but personal heartache, Shirley gave her heart and life to Jesus Christ. In search of the truth about the temperament theory, Shirley Ann Miller spent several years doing research, finding Biblical references, and examining over 300 resource books.

Today, Shirley's background as a Christian writer, and experience as a former professional astrologer, lend credibility to the unique perspective needed in explaining the relationship between the temperaments, the occult, and astrology. That is why she now brings you this book, TemperaMysticism.

Foreword

Shirley Ann Miller has done an inspired job of unmasking a major deception in the Church today—the spiritual application of the pseudo-psychological **temperament** theory for individual personality assessment. The author proves this teaching is not *new* at all, but is derived from ancient pagan and occultic philosophies.

Today, cloaked with seductive wrappings, study of the **temperaments** is offered to the unwitting as a sophisticated, almost magical way to understand our deepest natures and our personality *type*.

Shirley Ann Miller shows how far this humanistic teaching is from Biblical standards. She also explains exactly why it is absolutely essential that we abandon the man-centered, self-oriented, psycho-paganism of the **temperament** theory and rely *exclusively* for our life's direction on the unquestionably powerful direction of the *Holy Spirit*.

I highly recommend this book for anyone who truly desires to quicken one's discernment of the true things of God.

Texe Marrs

Introduction

Fascination with the occult, Satanism, witchcraft, and the New Age movement has steadily increased within the past twenty years. As part of this trend, there is a renewed interest in understanding the mysteries of the personality through the supernatural. This search to understand the personality has long been a part of secular society, but what is most alarming is the increased popularity of occult and New Age personality theories presently being introduced into the Christian community.

TemperaMysticism: The Truth About the Sanguine, Choleric, Phlegmatic, and Melancholy Personality Theory unveils the hidden meanings and previously untold facts regarding the temperament theory. Accepted and practiced by many Christians, the popularity of the temperament and other personality theories is increasing at an astounding rate. Are Christians unknowingly being lured into the occult by practicing the temperaments and other New Age personality typologies? The temperaments are being accepted so eagerly by many Christians that few have stopped to ask the underlying question, "Where did the temperaments originate?"

The fascinating study of people, their differences, individuality, and an acute interest in human nature led this writer into the world of astrology. Astrology appeared to offer answers into the intriguing mysteries and inner depths of the human personality.

Astrology categorizes people according to the month in which they were born, the minute, hour, and place where they were born. With its geometrical configurations, planetary positions, angles, etc., I pieced together a personality puzzle that appeared to work. Unfortunately, astrology attempts to fit square types of personalities where only the round type of personality fits. No matter how hard you try to force the square personality, it will never fit.

Astrological philosophy forces people to behave in a certain predictable pattern simply because of their birthday. Besides categorizing individuals into preprogrammed rules of conduct, astrology is intimately tied to the spirit world.

It all happened so innocently. One afternoon while browsing the shelves of a local bookstore, something caught my eye and also my curiosity. It was a book on astrology. Most 17 year olds similarly represent a sponge—soaking up everything of interest, especially if it's "in" or popular at the time. Well, I was your typical teenager and the subject of astrology simply fascinated me.

After studying the interesting and lively descriptions of different personalities, it was amazing how accurate the descriptions matched my family and friends. After that I began to read everything on astrology that was

INTRODUCTION

available. This was the beginning of my many years as a professional astrologer.

Astrology is divination; the "forthtelling" of time and destiny. Astrology is an ancient religion tied to the supernatural and the occult. While interpreting horoscopes, astrologers—even if they refuse to admit it—yield to a psychic transformation. They act as a "medium" between the higher spirit world of the universe and lower world of the earth.

As an astrologer I used a mystical, higher consciousness to tap into this spirit world. Because of the complexity and numerous ambiguities of the astrological chart, the astrologer must listen to the promptings of the "higher self." In this way, the astrologer can draw from spiritual guidance to counsel and direct the client. You might ask, "Who is the spiritual guide?" God does not work through astrology, therefore, these mystical, spiritual guides are in reality demonic spirits who freely give occult knowledge.

Astrologers have immense power over their clients; viewed as a sort of "cosmic magician" possessing secret, mystical inspiration from the heavens they relay future prognostications to an eager listener. Prognostication is an astrological term. It means to "predict" or "foretell" the future. Astrologers represent the "high priests of the universe."

In my desire to help people understand themselves and what was happening to them, I felt as if I sincerely offered a valuable service to mankind. Unfortunately, I didn't recognize the narrow-mindedness of categorizing people, placing them into a mold with little opportunity for understanding the unique God-given differences they have acquired as individuals. Nor was I aware of the deepening spiritual darkness that slowly encompassed my life.

For 12 years the occult world of astrology represented a part of my everyday existence. The ephemeris, zodiac, horoscopes, and occult books lined the shelves of my library. Many, many people filed through the door to have "the astrologer" predict their destiny and determine the outcome of future events.

People were interested in understanding themselves, their partners, their children, and also to know about career opportunities, health, and finances. Everyone asked questions about their future, and most importantly, expected me to have the answers.

One afternoon a lady walked into the office who traveled a very long distance for counseling. She was a small, quiet type of woman in her early thirties. As she sat in my office, I slowly constructed her astrological chart, piecing together all of the aspects of her personality.

We talked briefly, then suddenly she burst into tears. "I don't know what I'm going to do . . . . I can't stand this anymore! Please, please tell me what to do!" Startled by this unexpected outburst and weighted down with a great sense of responsibility, I knew she expected me to have all of the answers to solve her problems.

Peering into her chart I began to tell her in great detail about her past and future. Totally amazed at my perception, she began to calmly speak, "That's right! How did you know that?" On this very day, I asked myself this same question, *"How did* I know that?"

Why did I have this ability to "see" into someone's future? This so-called "talent" scared me more than ever before. It wasn't until now that I realized it wasn't me at all, but something or someone influencing me. Gradually it became apparent my whole existence was being controlled by something beyond me. Slowly, slowly my life spiraled downward. I desperately wanted

INTRODUCTION

out, but how? Then I cried out to God!

From the deepest pit God lifted me out and placed my feet upon solid ground. After many years of demonic captivity, heartache, and struggle, I found the Truth.

It's very difficult for anyone to escape the trappings of the occult, but nothing is impossible with God. After many years as a professional astrologer, Jesus Christ delivered me. Set free from the bondages of sin and heartache, I gave my heart and life to Jesus Christ.

Several years passed when a Christian friend gave me a book on the temperaments written by Tim LaHaye entitled, *Why You Act the Way You Do*. This book dealt with why people act the way they do because of the strengths and weaknesses of their temperament type. Christians were labeled a *sanguine, melancholy, choleric,* or *phlegmatic.*

After reading the book, memories of my days as a professional astrologer suddenly came to reality again. It was hard to believe, but the temperament classifications closely resembled the principles and terminology used in astrology. At one time these same temperament terms were used in my book manuscript based on the history and origins of astrology.

Again I discoverd the temperaments while visiting a local church. Glancing down it surprised me to see a temperament chart that a woman placed on the seat next to her. The chart was a page from a book by Florence Littauer entitled, *After Every Wedding Comes a Marriage*. It listed the four temperament names of sanguine, choleric, phlegmatic, and melancholy.[1]

Also, it seemed rather unusual to have a class on the temperaments being taught during the Sunday school hour. At this point, my thoughts were racing! What does the study of the temperaments have to do with the Bible and Sunday school?

TEMPERAMYSTICISM

When the Sunday school instructor was asked about the similarity between astrology and the temperaments, she replied that astrology represented the "false belief" and the temperaments were developed from the "truth" of God's Word so that Christians might understand their personalities. The instructor continued to explain, "After salvation a Christian's temperament becomes the Fruit of the Spirit."

Almost overnight the temperament teaching appeared on Christian television, radio, in retreats, Bible studies, and church services. Several years of gathering research on the occult origins of the temperaments resulted in this book. This information reflects the many hours of study combined with an extensive background and experience as a former professional astrologer.

Most importantly this book was written because of my belief in the Savior Jesus Christ. I am deeply grieved to think that an idolatrous form of astrology, which I happily left behind, is currently being infiltrated into Christian doctrine.

Is it possible for Christians to spiritually mature while studying worldly philosophies and doctrines? As Christians we must not accept teachings without first questioning the basic foundation and source of those teachings. Many times we may be so open to NEW things occurring in the church that we fail to question, "Is this teaching really from God?"

These are the last days. Satan knows his time is short. The deceiver is at work even in hopes of deceiving the very elect. Demonic spirits walk about laying their traps to catch undiscerning Christians. God's word has not changed and His truths have not changed. Everything we think must filter from our thoughts through the truth of the Word of God. Satan wants carnal believers so the Holy Spirit is quenched and

INTRODUCTION

to confuse the leading of God. To examine and test our walk is a very important element in following the Spirit of God. We must examine all thoughts and feelings which come to us in order to discern whether these originate from God, from ourself, or from Satan.

The Holy Spirit intentionally gives believers the ability to discern any teaching or circumstance that enters their life. We must be sensitive to the Holy Spirit to hear Him speaking to us in our daily walk. Without his guidance, we can easily stumble and fall prey to Satan's deceptive tactics.

Today's scientific and medical discoveries are based upon the failings and findings of our ingenious ancestors; therefore, it is most important not to discredit their vast contributions to society. When we accept scripturally-based teachings, though, we must be certain those same teachings originate from the Bible and from those who believe in the Lord Jesus Christ. Christianity is not a psychological experience but a spiritual transformation.

Although I do not agree with the temperament teachings of Tim LaHaye and Florence Littauer, it is my belief they truly are genuine, sincere Christians whose motive is to encourage and help others. This is true with most of the authors and teachers of the temperaments who earnestly pursue the study of the temperaments as a tool for self-understanding. Tragically, though, there is a mixing of temperament and personality teachers who are not Christian but represent the New Age guru whose desire is blinded by New Age systems and worldly philosophies. Deceptive teachings are purposely being introduced into Biblical doctrine to lead Christians away from the truth.

TEMPERAMYSTICISM

Many Christian books written on coping are encouraging, uplifting, and spiritually inspiring. Unfortunately, numerous New Age books are also appearing on the shelves of Christian bookstores which contain worldly wisdom based upon human tradition and values rather than the Word of God.

Hopefully, this book will present another side to the issue of the four temperaments so that Christians may compare these facts from a Biblical perspective. In comparing Biblical references to historical accounts, hopefully we as Christians will be able to piece together the temperament puzzle to discover the truth.

From most historical accounts, the temperament humouralists (as the temperament theorists were called) were men of philosophy, humanistic in their theories; these ancient Greek philosophers practiced a religious philosophy which incorporated all of nature as "god." Because the ancient pagan civilizations believed in many gods they failed to recognize the one true God, and developed religious theories which satisfied their lust for self-knowledge. The religion of the Graeco-Roman world was anti-Christ. Philosophers considered the "mind" and philosophy as the window to the eternal soul. The polytheistic Graeco-Roman world desperately searched for God and struggled to find the truth. Oblivious to the frailties and weaknesses found in the human character, philosophy held that man was god. Man was the totality of power, controlling his destiny and fate.

Somewhere within the last 30 years a growing number of Christians have become entangled in these ancient and medieval personality systems: the temperaments, astrology, the enneagram, phrenology, and graphology, among others. Whatever the label of the New Age personality system, its origins can be traced to ancient philosophy or occult religions.

The recent introduction of the temperament theory into the Christian church should in itself raise some important spiritual questions. Is the popular temperament movement compatible with Christian beliefs and practices? Is the temperament philosophy Christian revelation or New Age deception? The answer to these questions can be found in the Bible as well as in the archives of ancient historical references, even those in existence before the birth of Jesus Christ. This book addresses these issues by revealing the mysterious origins of this philosophy unveiling the real definitions of the temperament terminology. Because of the subtle influence of this philosophy and the obscure meanings of the temperament names, it is most important for Christians to discern the underlying occult connection.

In reading this book on the temperaments, we as Christians must realize that this is not an attack on the credibility of Christian brothers and sisters, but a realization that these are the end times and all doctrine must be weighed and measured in light of the Gospel of Jesus Christ. Hopefully, this research will be of benefit to the reader. More importantly, as Paul wrote:

> *For the time will come when they will not endure sound doctrine; but after their own lusts shall they heap to themselves teachers, having itching ears; And they shall turn away their ears from the truth, and shall be turned unto fables* (II Timothy 4:3-4).

1

The Temperaments

> *Their sorrows shall be multiplied that hasten after another god: their drink offerings of blood will I not offer, nor take up their names into my lips.*
> Psalm 16:4

Phlegmatic, sanguine, choleric, and melancholy: Do they sound like strange, eerie words? Do they have equally mysterious meanings? Perhaps the difficulty lies in the effort to pronounce them or how the words stick to the tongue when spoken rather than flow effortlessly from the lips. Nevertheless, these four unusual words describe a "new" revelation and overnight sensation currently exerting a powerful influence on Christianity. The phlegmatic, sanguine, choleric, and melancholy terms are more commonly known as the "temperaments."

The temperaments have found Christianity, or rather is it that Christianity has found the temperaments? The temperament philosophy came from relative obscurity only to be recently resurrected into a full-fledged, passionately-loved system of belief.

One Christian after another will testify, "The temperaments have changed my life! Now I'm able to understand myself and others much better!"

Over and over again Christians proclaim the seemingly miraculous effects the temperaments have had on their lives. What about the transformation the Holy Spirit brings into one's life at salvation? Once upon a time, Christians sang praises to Jesus Christ. Now instead many sing praise to the transforming power of the temperaments. What bewitching fascination do the temperaments possess holding many captive to its mysterious terminology and ambiguous personality descriptions?

It appears that just a small number of temperament authors and teachers have managed to convince a vast, growing number of people that this philosophy is a worthwhile spiritual belief. The temperaments have caused a spiritual chain reaction touching the lives of one person after another. What are the temperaments? Where did the terminology originate? What do the temperament terms really mean?

Temperament vs. The Temperaments

The *temperament* might be defined as the unique mental and emotional disposition identifiable as the personality. On the other hand, the *temperaments* classify personality traits, dividing, categorizing, and grouping them into one of four character or "temperament" types: sanguine, choleric, phlegmatic, or melancholy.

The temperament is a description of the personality in general, while the temperaments specifically classify character traits into a four-fold description of the personality. According to the temperament teachers, this theory identifies the true nature of the personality.

THE TEMPERAMENTS

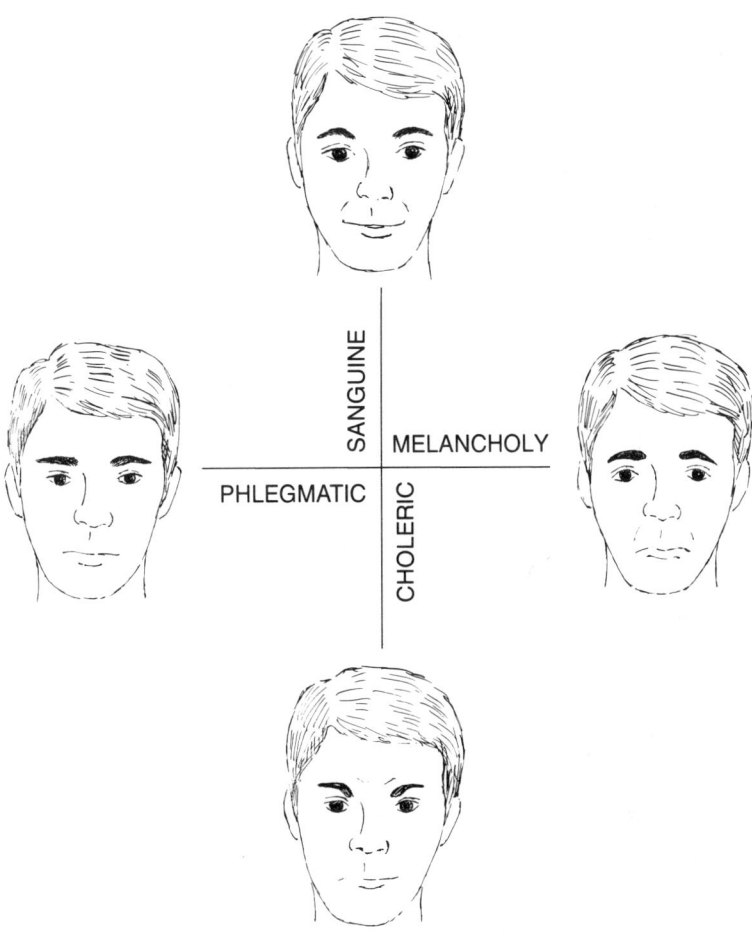

Eric Fromm (1900-1980) defined the personality as "the totality of inherited and acquired psychic qualities which are characteristic of one individual and which make the individual unique."[1] He further stated;

> "While differences in temperament have no ethical significance, differences in character constitute the real problem of ethics; they are expressive of the degree to which an individual has succeeded in the art of living."[2]

How Does a Christian Determine His Temperament Type?

The basic temperament type is determined by a simple test listing both positive and negative word descriptions describing personality traits. These positive and negative words describe character *strengths* and *weaknesses*. The temperament student selects the words most closely resembling his personality. The words are then compiled and separated under the four temperament names. The category with the most personality traits indicated the appropriate temperament type.

According to the temperament philosophy, a Christian is classified predominately as one particular character type (for example, a sanguine). Because of the complexities of the personality, however, temperament teachers explain that individuals are more than likely a combination of two of the temperament types, such as a sanguine-choleric. There are approximately 12 different temperament combinations possible to explain a person's temperament type. As I will explain in later chapters, these same 12 temperament combinations (known as triplicities) are identical to the personality descriptions used in professional astrology.

Why Do Christians Practice the Temperament Theory?

At this point you may ask, "What do you mean practice the temperaments? We don't practice the temperaments, the temperaments represent my true personality! They explain why I act the way I do!"

According to the temperament philosophy, identification of the temperament type(s) is the first step in the process of understanding the personality. Apparently knowledge of the temperament type magically opens the door to self-understanding, revealing the true nature of the personality with its strengths and weaknesses. The result of this deeper understanding of the self is in actuality the acknowledgement of whether a Christian is good (strength) or if they are mostly bad (weakness).

The temperament philosophy strives to promote harmonious relationships in marriage, in the home, in the work environment, and in all facets of life through compatibility and the understanding of differences. Temperament followers claim acknowledgement of the temperament differences results in achieving greater harmony and interaction in personal relationships. Ideally, this sounds wonderful and is something everyone should seek to attain in their relationship with others.

On the surface, the temperament philosophy appears to be a beneficial tool used in interacting with others. Naturally, everyone desires to maintain a balance and harmony in their interpersonal relationships. Friction and tension on a continual basis results in divorce, stress, illness, and heartache.

The Claims and Contradictions of the Temperament Theory

After identifying the temperament type and its associated strengths and weaknesses, the next step taught by temperament teachers is to learn how to overcome weaknesses by turning them into strengths. At this point, the temperament theory is interspersed with scripture, specifically the Holy Spirit's power and the Fruit of the Spirit (Galatians 5:22-23). In this way temperament teachers explain how Christians, by overcoming weaknesses, can reach their highest potential in spirit, soul, and body. Unfortunately, combining scriptural references with the temperament theory is in essence a "Christianization" of the temperaments; it is an attempt to lend credibility to this theory, thereby granting the temperaments the "stamp of approval."

Florence Littauer in her book, *Personality Plus* states:

> "As we each aim to improve our personalities, we can hope to exhibit the fruit of the Spirit in our lives."[3]

This explanation is consistent in all of her books regarding the temperaments. A closer look at what the Bible reveals would tell Christians differently. We don't exhibit the Fruit of the Spirit by improving our personalities, the Fruit of the Spirit shines forth because we possess the fullness of the Holy Spirit of God. The carnal personality has nothing to do with the Fruit of the Spirit. The Fruit of the Holy Spirit represents the personality or character of Christ.

Florence Littauer also states:

> "The study of the temperaments enables Christians to get a deeper understanding of the real you . . . ."[4]

then quotes John 16:13. *When he, the Spirit of truth shall come, he will guide you into all truth . . . .* Jesus wasn't speaking of the knowledge of your personality characteristics or temperaments as the truth. Jesus told of the Holy Spirit's guidance "into all truth" regarding Himself. The truth is the word of God, not the temperaments. "The real you" is the spirit man. Jesus Christ through the power of the Holy Spirit shining forth through you.

The temperament doctrine is rampantly spreading throughout Christianity from California to New York, from the Northern states to the deep South, influencing all denominations, and competing with the Bible as a study tool for spiritual growth. Temperament and personality books line the shelves of Christian bookstores. Christians are taking classes in churches and seminars to discover their temperament type, labeling each other according to the temperament names but totally unaware of the significant spiritual dangers lurking in the shadows of this seemingly innocent philosophical jargon.

Initially, temperament teachers caution their students to use the temperaments selectively; then contradicting themself, they proceed to explain how to categorically type people in all personal interactions whether they are family, business, or social relationships. Temperament followers rely almost completely on their basic understanding of temperament strengths/weaknesses in determining compatibility with others. In fact, people are labled so indiscriminately that when a pronounced strength/weakness is exhibited in the personality, instantly temperament enthusiasts categorize that person in one of the four temperament classifications. For example, a boldly decisive person becomes angry using sharp, cutting remarks. That person is immediately placed in predominantly the choleric temperament stating they behaved this way *because they are a choleric*. Rather than simply possessing an uncontrollable temper and totally operating from the flesh, that person is labeled a choleric because of their actions.

This inconsistent process of superficially classifying Christian's personalities into one of the four temperaments is like a spiritual cancer spreading from one church to another. This casual observance of personalities brings to memory a time twenty years ago when the most popular question to ask was, "What is your astrology sign?" Today, it is a different question. Many Christians are asking, "What is your temperament type?"

Do The Temperaments Place the Holy Spirit in a Secondary Position?

Temperament teachers explain that knowledge of the temperament weaknesses enable Christians, with the help of the Holy Spirit, to transform them into strengths. This idea appears to be a valid argument in favor of the temperaments; however, agreement with this idea implies an acknowledgement of the validity of the temperament theory as a viable "truth" for Christians to follow. **The temperament theory is in actuality a "false truth," leading many down the road towards deception.**

If you look closely at the temperament strengths and weaknesses, you will notice that none of the Fruit of the Spirit is listed. This is because the strengths and weaknesses are by-products of the flesh. As Christians aren't we supposed to produce Fruit? For instance, people can love in their flesh nature but God produces the agape, eternal love which is part of His spiritual nature and not the temporal love of the carnal nature.

The Bible teaches in Galatians 5:16-17, . . . *Walk in the Spirit, and ye shall not fulfil the lust of the flesh.* The necessity of knowing a particular temperament type is not mentioned in the Bible as the primary transforming power of the fleshly nature. In fact, no reference to the temperaments can be found anywhere in scripture. Rather it is the Holy Spirit of God who is our source of power, enabling a Christian to overcome the weaknesses of the flesh, *For the flesh lusteth against the Spirit, and the Spirit against the flesh* . . . (Galatians 5:17). We are told in Galatians 5:24, 25, *And they that are Christ's have crucified the flesh . . . . If we live in the Spirit, let us also walk in the Spirit* by sacrificing the fleshly nature (personality or temperament), submitting to God in prayer and obedience, and knowing the Word of God.

THE TEMPERAMENTS

In contrast, **the temperament theory teaches reliance on the self as the foremost power to change the personality, and second, the Holy Spirit and the Word of God.** The power to transform weaknesses into strengths is solely based on the acknowledgement of the appropriate temperament classification. Also, by saying this theory is recognized by modern medicine and even as a part of Christian doctrine, temperament teachers are establishing the temperaments as a valid theory to use in self-understanding.

The powers of the self such as: self-love, esteem, knowledge, and understanding are given preeminence over the power of the Holy Spirit to change a person's inner being. Only the Lord can change a person from the inside out. The temperament concept works in reverse, attempting to change a person from the outside in.

The Spiritual Danger Behind the Temperaments

On the surface the temperament teachers do not appear to be saying anything unscriptural. In fact, the temperament philosophy, blended with Scripture, is utilized as a simplified way to explain the many mysteries of the personality. Tragically, this false teaching is infiltrating the true teachings of the Word of God. If indeed the temperament teaching is erroneous, then the real meaning and practice of the temperaments must be revealed. Has Christianity overlooked the underlying, destructive work of the temperaments because this personality theory is interspersed with scripture?

Satan is very good at masquerading his lies, and it is easier than we think for him to *transform into an angel of light* (II Corintians 11:14). He is comparable to the termite in wood; sometimes you don't know he's there until the wall collapses.

The temperament theory is spreading throughout Christianity as if it were some new revelation from the Bible which has laid dormant for thousands of years, only to be suddenly revealed to Christians. In fact, temperament enthusiasts are so adamant and defensive about the temperaments they actually believe the temperament theory is from God because it is used with the Bible. If this be the case, what temperament was the first man, Adam? Was Adam a sanguine, choleric, phlegmatic, or melancholy? If he was of the phlegmatic temperament, then when did the other three enter the picture? Adam would have been a rather confused individual lacking a complete personality. If God created man in His image, then what temperament is God?

Temperament teachers explain to me that Jesus Christ represented a combination of all four of the temperaments. He possessed all of the strengths but none of the weaknesses. Where is the scriptural linkage between Christ and the temperaments? In other words, temperament teachers place the Creator in a temperament box. He is thus limited by the boundaries of His creation. The temperaments place fleshly principles upon the divine nature of Christ. *We are the circumcision, which worship God in the spirit, and rejoice in Christ Jesus, and have no confidence in the flesh* (Philippians 3:3).

Do you see how this process of casually labeling Christians is totally absurd! Rather than following the inspired writings of the prophets and New Testament teachers to mature spiritually, the entire Christian community is slowly being spoon-fed and programmed into believing a recently introduced philosophy which has no basis in Christianity.

Many Christians have found the temperament theory

THE TEMPERAMENTS

to be extremely fascinating, if not addicting. The mysterious and intriguing sense of "self-discovery" has undoubtedly contributed to the overall excitement generated because of this "new" personality system.

The fact is the temperament theory is only new for the Christian. The temperament theory initially belonged only to the ancient Greek philosophers. Temperament authors claim the temperament theory began over 2,000 years ago during the time of Hippocrates. Actually, the temperament philosophy initially came into being hundreds of years *before* Hippocrates. The Hippocratic writings only expounded on the temperament philosophy giving it the necessary "push" into prominence. As a result, the temperament philosophy would become the common acceptable form of belief for hundreds of years afterward.

Within the Christian community, though, the temperament system has gained significance only within the last 30 years. What is even more alarming is the fact that the recent emergence of the temperament philosophy coincides with the resurging interest in astrology and other New Age personality systems.

According to the Bible, God's Word is forever (Matthew 24:35) and unchanging, thus any new doctrines introduced to the Christian should be judged according to scripture. The Word of God reveals truth and the Holy Spirit leads and guides believers into all truth and knowledge regarding the wisdom of God. Instead of searching the scriptures for themselves, Christians rely totally on pastors, teachers, and evangelists to do the study work for them, and many of these leaders teach the temperaments based upon what someone else has written. You see what is wrong with this? Everyone is trusting what others say without studying the Bible for themself to see if the temperament teaching is really scriptural.

No reference to the temperaments is given in the Bible. The temperament theorists, on the other hand, strongly promote the temperament concept in an attempt to convince Christians that the temperament theory is part of scripture. If the temperaments were such an important part of our spiritual growth, why are they not mentioned in the Word of God? For example, temperament teachers explain that Paul represented the choleric temperament because of his bold, decisive nature. **If the temperaments were so important in identifying the fleshly nature of the apostles or prophets, perhaps Romans Chapter 1:1 would have read, "Paul, a Choleric and servant of Jesus Christ . . . ." Instead, Paul exclaimed, "Not I, but Christ!"**

Paul's teachings emphasized the spiritual man and not the fleshly person. Christians are to . . . *present your bodies a living sacrifice, holy, acceptable unto God . . . . And be not conformed to this world: but be ye transformed by the renewing of your mind* . . . (Romans 12:1-2).

The temperaments appeal to the logical reasoning of the mind. The mind isn't transformed by knowledge of the temperaments. The mind is renewed and transformed by the Word of God! **It is more important to know the spiritual nature of men in the Bible rather than determining their temperament type.** It is also more important to know the spiritual nature of Christians rather than improving or understanding what temperament type they are.

The temperament theory is promoted so intensely and temperament teachers labor so passionately to "sell" the idea of the temperaments that this theory is virtually accepted throughout Christianity without anyone stopping to investigate its origins. The heavy

THE TEMPERAMENTS

advertising and promotion of the temperaments in churches all over the country is evidence of the popularity and acceptance of this philosophy. The temperament fever is raging and temperament enthusiasm is spreading so rapidly, that it is very difficult for Christians to slow down. It is time for the Body of Christ to pause for prayer, discernment, and understanding in regards to this ancient philosophical doctrine.

It is my concern that the proponents of the temperament theory have not investigated any farther back in time than Hippocrates and, therefore, do not understand the mythical, astrological, and anti-Christ origins of the temperament theory.

Temperament followers claim the temperaments maintain a natural, physical truth. Oddly, I found astrology maintains this exact same appearance. The temperaments relate very closely to the divination practiced in astrology. Isn't "foretelling the future" also predicting actions based upon which temperament type one is? In other words, it is thought a melancholy will act a certain way because of the fact that they are considered a melancholy temperament type. Astrology claims you will act a certain way because you were born in a particular sign of the constellation. Just because something *works* doesn't necessarily mean it is from God. Astrology belongs to the secular, occult world and the temperaments are intimately associated with Christianity.

Christian temperament teachers explain to me that the temperaments are God's answer to the "horriblescope" (astrological horoscope). This cannot be true because both astrology and the temperaments are branches of the same tree—ancient Babylon.

At this point in Biblical history when we draw closer to the imminent return of Jesus Christ, one of the greatest concerns for Christians should be, "Why the sudden interest in the temperament personality theory?" Perhaps this fascination and acceptance of the temperaments is associated with the great falling away mentioned in the Bible (II Thessalonians 2:3). A slow, subtle turning away from the truths of the Bible. Christians enticed with worldly philosophies do not have their hearts and minds on Jesus Christ.

The Acceptance of Ancient Philosophical Theories

Because of the increasing acceptance of the temperament personality theory and its present rate of growth, many Christians will be indoctrinated, or at the very least vaguely familiar, with this theory within the next few years.

Before we accept new theories being introduced into Biblical curriculums, we must question their origins. Unfortunately, this is not the approach taken with the temperament theory. At the present time, the temperament theory is being welcomed as an integral part of many church educational studies and taught in Sunday school classes, church groups, singles fellowships, Christian retreats, and other Bible-oriented groups. Without testing and questioning the Biblical basis of different theories, how can we know if they should be applied to the spiritual life of a Christian? Everything must be weighed and examined in comparison to God's Word.

People today are searching for peace, harmony, and personal satisfaction. Twenty years ago, society placed greater emphasis on values, morals, and ethics based upon family traditions which passed from one generation to the next. Simple ways of life gave way to busy, stress-filled days where family values and customs have almost been eliminated. People search everywhere for happiness, contentment, and a peaceful heart.

Society has changed; peace, love, and tranquility are now pursued through drugs, sex, secular humanism, and the occult. The god of "self" and his child "selfishness" have slowly emerged. Many people religiously worship the self by practicing various forms of idolatry through the occult such as psychic power, witchcraft, inner consciousness, meditation, holistic and universalistic thought, and other ways of self-adoration. The god of self continually searches the depths of human consciousness to find an end to the inner search for tranquility.

This is the church's finest hour. Today's search for spiritualism opens an unprecedented opportunity for a believer to present the gospel. Jesus Christ is the answer to a world full of anxiety, sorrow, and discouragement. People are asking questions, they want to know the truth, and these questions can be answered in the truth of the gospel of Jesus Christ.

This opportunity, which is unparalleled in history, must not be stolen because the god of self entered into the hearts of Christians everywhere. Christians are a people set apart, not to be contaminated by worldly wisdoms and philosophies. The words of Jesus remain unadulterated, pure in truth and wisdom, not watered down with human traditions or the religiosity of the world. At present we must ask ourselves, "Is the temperament theory a part of the religiosity of the world, or does the temperament theory bring us into a closer relationship with God?"

2
The New Age Movement, Christians, And The Temperaments

"Every man, however good, has yet a better man within him. When the outer man is unfaithful to his deeper convictions, the hidden man whispers a protest. The name of the whisper in the soul is conscience."[1]

Friedrich Heinrich Alexander Von Humboldt

Satan's Disguise

Satan is knocking on the door of the church. His polished appearance and smooth style conceal thousands of years of practicing deception. Dressed in an obviously expensive, well-tailored business suit made of the very finest material, he is unpretentious, extremely polite, and disarmingly courteous; not what one might expect from someone with his reputation.

This super salesman is offering his newest product for sale called "The New Age Movement." Being a slick con man, he deliberately failed to mention to his prospective buyer that his hot little product is not new but rather a repackaged version of an old, outdated philosophy which he sold over 2,000 years ago. Tragically, many Christians listen to his smooth sales talk, succumbing to his captivating words they innocently buy his bag of goodies. This may sound shocking but actually this is the real picture of the New Age Movement and its attempt to infiltrate into Christianity.

One of the tools Satan uses to deceive is to attempt to merge deceptive doctrines and practices into Christian beliefs. Satan *adds* to the word of God. Eventually the Bible isn't enough to satisfy the thirst for wisdom and guidance. It becomes necessary to utilize an additional study tool to read side-by-side with the Bible. All of this is done so subtley that undiscerning Christians may accept these study tools as Biblical-based rather than recognizing this as a deceptive weapon used by Satan to slowly draw Christians away from the truth of God's word. Satan masterfully leads the way in a continual search for carnal satisfaction to calm a disruptive conscience.

The New Age Philosophy

Most of the New Age Movement is universally appealing, offering peace and hope to a troubled world. Hope, peace, truth, and love are all sought by New Age followers. All of this is thought to be found residing in the deepest, inner core of the human being. The highest, single goal of the New Age philosophy is an attempt to rebuild the inner man through stepping stones of higher consciousness eventually reaching the elevated pinnacle of self—the god within. This is the deceptive teaching of spiritualism, "a form of godliness."

New Age followers respect nature and all that is created, yet they fail to recognize the Creator. Sadly, the New Agers have left out the "Prince of Peace" Himself, Jesus Christ. All other forms of peace, faith, and hope are on a temporal basis which is dependent upon the mood of the moment, or an eventful happening that temporarily offers an exciting change from a boring worldly existence.

Denying the divinity of Jesus Christ, the New Agers believe that a god is the summation of all that exists. God is seen as a great impersonal "force" or energy which encompasses all of life, and His name is used merely as an expression to describe the totality of mankind or "wholeness" with nature.

As the force within the universe, god is supposedly a great energy pattern made up of molecules and microbes spinning and traveling through space and at some point "banging" into one another, creating a new planet or creature in the universe.

Wholistic thought encompasses all of nature harmonizing with the inner spiritual world expressed through man to the outer physical world. Thus, New Age followers seek to attain "harmony" inside the body first which results in harmony within the universe. The universe, they feel, is ruled by certain fixed laws whereby even "the god of force" cannot change and is bound, moving and operating within a natural sphere of existence never changing and forever "being."

New Agers worship the *totality of the universe* as a god rather than God as the *Creator of the universe*. As Paul said, *Who changed the truth of God into a lie, and worshipped and served the creature more than the Creator* . . . (Romans 2:25).

History Repeats Itself

The New Age Movement is actually the reshaping of history from the "ancient age" to present history. The New Age is a repeat of ancient and medieval civilization where, to the pagan, "self" was god. When the self was united with nature the person then became whole, or god. Therefore, as a god the person was entitled to eternal life and all of the other privileges the status of divinity might afford.

The ultimate purpose of ancient philosophy and the current New Age Movement is to reach a "higher self" which is comparable to a place of divinity. The way to a higher self is a process of transformation from the physical to the spiritual nature. New Agers believe this process can only be reached through a state of higher consciousness. As a result meditation, astral projection, reincarnation, ascended masters, astrology, witchcraft, visualization, hypnosis, and other methods are used to escape the mundane home of the physical by plummeting one's self into the depths of the unknown.

The spiritual world is real and the New Agers have their "antennas up" in hopes of tapping into it. Unfortunately, by dabbling in this occult spiritual world they fall prey to a variety of demonic influences and seducing spirits which more than welcome the chance to possess and control a human being.

Satan desires to spiritually separate mankind from God and to keep the Christian out of continued fellowship with God. He does this by destroying confidence in God and in His word through sin, doubt, and unbelief. Faith is given by the Holy Spirit and will grow only when closely cherished.

Satan is definitely determined to destroy the Christian. What better way than to walk innocently into the

Christian church with his ancient philosophies repackaged attractively to fit the Christian's doctrinal point of view: "Christian, may I introduce the temperaments?"

The Church Needs Discernment

Today, more than ever before, the Christian needs discernment. For a world turned upside down, inside out, and topsy turvy, Christians must discern the "true" from the "false." Within the next few years a barrage of New Age thinking will attempt to force its way into church doctrine. If Christians allow even one part of New Age thinking to become an integral part of Biblical doctrine, other deceptive teaching will surely follow. It is important for Christians to *put on the armor of God* to combat this invasion of New Age teaching now and conquer it before it gains a foothold in the church and in the lives of Christians.

Most of the time deceptive doctrine is very subtle, as false teachings are often mixed with the truth. Satan unveils this counterfeit which so nearly resembles the truth that it snares those who are willing to be deceived. **It is impossible, though, for Satan to hold one Christian under his power who earnestly seeks to know the truth.**

Many philosophical doctrines may give the appearance of wisdom and truth while in actuality they are a lie. Satan's skillful scripture strategy is to place his own interpretation upon passages hoping to cause us to stumble. The temperaments offer this mask of truth.

In all appearances the temperaments offer a solution to the mystery of the personality. Herein lies the enigma. Without being defensive or angry Christians must research where the temperaments originated: God, man or Satan?

If the temperament theory is from God, then scripture will confirm its teachings revealing the truth. Jesus Christ is the truth and *the light which lighteth every man that cometh into the world* (John 1:9). The Holy Spirit has been sent to guide Christians into all truth. *If any man will do his will, he shall know of the doctrine, whether it be of God, or whether I speak of myself* (John 7:17).

If the temperament theory is not from God but from man, it will oppose the basic doctrines of Christianity representing the spirit of the world and Satan, holding the elements of truth, convincingly sprinkled in with scripture to make it believable to undiscerning Christians. Undoubtedly, what better way to convince Christians of the temperament's credibility than to learn the theory from other Christians. Satan has a great networking plan!

The Self As God

Both the New Age Movement and the temperaments place spiritual emphasis on the "self." In an effort to reach the highest potential, these philosophies teach worldly principles of self-understanding, self-love, and self-esteem. As a result, the self is placed in a position of divinity which ultimately becomes idolatry. As stated in Romans 10:3:

> *For they being ignorant of God's righteousness, and going about to establish their own righteousness, have not submitted themselves unto the righteousness of God.*

The New Age Movement and the temperaments teach deceptive doctrines which place emphasis on the self rather than the person of Jesus Christ. The New Age Movement excludes God totally, and the temperaments psychoanalyze the nature of the Fruit of the Holy Spirit. The Fruit does not originate in the carnal, philosophical, or psychological nature of man but comes from God. Both theories express a form of freedom in spirituality; actually, they place a person in bondage to their sinful, fleshly nature.

Someone once mentioned, the center of sin is "I." Every form of strife and dissension are rooted in the "self" nature. We sin because our human nature is sinful. Only Jesus Christ in His selfless incarnate love can set us free from the bondage of self.

The selfless nature of Christ is to be vulnerable. An openness to love and forgiveness is vulnerability as a strength rather than as a weakness. To be willing to give in, or even to lose, is surrendering in strength and leading in weakness. It takes more strength and self-control to yield, resisting the self-nature so that Christ's nature through the Holy Spirit will emerge. Every time we surrender in strength, while leading in weakness, character building attributes attach to our personality. As a result, we mature spiritually. We grow more Christlike. This is because our strengths reside in Jesus Christ (Psalm 18:2, 28:7, 27:1, 46:1, 81:1, Philemon 4:13, I Peter 5:10). In Christ when *we are weak, we are strong* (I Corinthians 4:10).

Sadly, though, the coming trend in Christianity is not self-denial, humiliation, or sacrifice. The doctrines that many find the most favorable are the ones less spiritual, satisfying the "itching ears" and the hungers of the soul. *Never* are we so wise as to avoid searching the Bible in earnest prayer for divine guidance. The Holy Spirit reveals to our spiritual nature the will of God which, when obeyed, brings spiritual maturity manifesting outwardly through our personality.

3

Where Did The Temperaments Originate?

" . . . For a physician who is a lover of wisdom is the equal of a god."[1]

"Decorum" C. Kerenyi

According to Christian temperament teachers, the temperament theory's philosophy was conceived by Hippocrates over 2000 years ago. Historically, though, Hippocrates was not the person who developed the original philosophy of the temperaments. He borrowed this teaching from a man named Empedocles. By combining Empedocles' teachings and his own theories, Hippocrates formed his theory of the temperaments which is currently being practiced by Christians today.

Do Christians who apply the temperament theory to their spiritual life and Biblical doctrine know the spiritual beliefs of the men from whom this theory originated? To Biblically correlate this teaching, one might say that Hippocrates and his predecessors represent the prophets, and those who apply these teachings their disciples. Did these ancient teachers know Jehovah God? Obviously not, since Hippocrates and his predecessors were Greek philosophers who rejected the writings of Moses and the Old Testament prophets. If these philosophers did not know Jehovah God, then who or what did they worship?

Hippocrates and Asclepius

Hippocrates was a philosopher and physician born in Greece on the island of Cos (off the West coast of Asia Minor) around 460 B.C. He was portrayed as a mythological god-like figure amidst the backdrop of ancient Greece.

Hippocrates' use of simple therapeutic practices and his philosophical observance of the sick gained him the name "The Father of Medicine" and he reigned as the foremost scientific authority until the Nineteenth Century. The 70 works attributed to him were most likely written by students of the Hippocrates School of Medicine and titled *The Hippocratic Collection.*

In Hippocrates' time medicine closely resembled a mixture of religion, magic, astrology, omens, and superstition. The island of Cos, Hippocrates' birthplace, eventually became a central location for the study of astrology. Berosus, a Chaldean priest of Baal, established a school on the island to teach his students the occult arts of astrology and divination. The common philosophy of ancient Greece held that the study of astrology was a prerequisite to the practice of medicine.

WHERE DID THE TEMPERAMENTS ORIGINATE?

Hippocrates, the son of Heracleides a descendant of Hercules, intimately associated with a group of priest-physicians called the Asclepiades. These were the selected few who, by heritage or eminent birth, were initiated into the ancient secret wisdoms of Asclepius, the son of Apollo and mythical god of alchemy and medicine.

Hippocrates pursued his early medical training in the temples of the Asclepius cult. According to *Asklepios, Archetypal Image of the Physician's Existence* by C. Kerenyi, Asclepius was "the god of physicians."[2]

The Asclepius cult originated at Tricca (in Thessaly). The god-physician Asclepius supposedly lived during the Twelfth Century B.C.; during that time the gods bestowed upon him the gift of healing. After his death, around the Fifth or Sixth Century, the mythical gods elevated Asclepius to a position of divinity; eventually he became the most prominently worshipped deity of the ancient pagan world.

The Greeks believed disease, sickness, and destiny were completely in the hands of their gods.[3] The gods were thought to personally interact with mortals on earth to bring good or evil. An angry god would send various diseases through demon spirits. The pagan follower could be set free from these demonic spirits only through a process of prayer, cleansing, sacrifice and purification.[4]

Asclepius worship eventually spread throughout all of ancient civilization. To the pagan world and Hippocrates, Asclepius was thought to be the savior of the world.[5] As Henry Sigerist explains in *A History of Medicine,*

> "... in this multitude of divine healers one gradually stood out; one became the leading healing deity, eclipsing Apollo himself; one came

to be worshipped universally on the mainland . . . one healing god became so powerful that when Christianity entered the world as a religion that promised healing and redemption, he, of all pagan gods, was the only serious competitor of Christ. This was Asclepius."[6]

Asclepius worship represented the epitome of the ancient civilizations' idolatrous beliefs. In one of the Hippocratic writings, the author expressed his belief in the gods and human interactions with them: "Prayer indeed is good, but while calling on the gods a man should himself lend a hand."[7] Perhaps this is the original ancient translation of a phrase which has passed through history only to be Christianized in its final form of God helps those who are willing to help themselves.

At some point in time, the ancient dieties were thought to have existed in the physical, earthly world (anthropomorphic). This mythical hierarchy represented a touchable, lifegiving, symbolic godhead possessing a variety of tangible shapes and forms. After death those destined for immortality became a god assuming a position of authority over humanity to rule and reign in their lofty kingdom above the earth.

The Dream Cure of Asclepius

The healing god Asclepius appeared in the temple during the night and always through dreams. The ancient philosophers thought dreams were produced by spirits. The mind was considered to be divine, therefore all thoughts were associated with divine direction. At night when the soul is quieted during sleep a spirit sent messages that moved upward through the body to the brain. The messages relayed the spirit's guidance for healing, direction, or to recall some forgotten experience. Every dream, however, was thought to be from a god and thus a significant part of the pagan worshipper's existence.

Approximately two hundred temples were dedicated to Asclepius throughout the Graeco-Roman empire. The most famous of these is Epidauros, where the name Drako "the snake" became a significant part of Asclepius worship, and where a statue of Asclepius rests seated on his throne with a staff in one hand and the other over the head of a serpent.[8]

Within the temple of Asclepius sat an altar and also a stoa (a portico) for the practice of encoemesis or ritual incubation (the dream cure). The patient visited the temple at night to experience a drug induced sleep causing them to dream. This became the vehicle by which the god Asclepius advised the patient regarding a prescribed treatment.

Dreams and also the snake held a close association with the gods of the underworld. The underworld was believed to be the symbolic representation of the unconscious mind. Dreams were thought to be the mysterious intervention of the gods who instructed and directed mortals in living their earthly life. The ancient Graeco-Roman world worshipped the snake as the healing symbol of Asclepius. In contrast, the Bible speaks of the snake as . . . *that old serpent, called the Devil and Satan, which deceiveth the whole world . . .* (Revelations 12:9).

The priest-physician representing the god Asclepius performed surgery, medical techniques, and applied herbal remedies. During his nightly visits while the patient was dreaming, the priest-physician brought with him snakes who supposedly nursed the patient's wounds. In the morning, the patient's dream would be explained by a prophet, diviner, or dream interpreter to determine Asclepius' will for present or future events.

Unless given by God to the prophets, the interpretation of dreams was forbidden in the Old Testament, even if they came to pass, because the surrounding people would *entice thee secretly, saying, Let us go and serve other gods* . . . (Deuteronomy 13:6). The false prophets did not speak God's word, but prophesied lies to deceive the children of the Lord and lead them into idolatry. They spoke *the vision of their own heart, and not out of the mouth of the Lord* (Jeremiah 15:16).

> *If there arise among you a prophet, or a dreamer of dreams, and giveth thee a sign or a wonder . . . . Thou shalt not hearken unto the words of that prophet, or that dreamer of dreams: for the Lord your God proveth you* . . . (Deuteronomy 13:1-3).

Asclepius, Ancient Medicine, and Religion

From the earliest records, the practice of medicine ran a parallel course with religion. Sigerist in *A History of Medicine* notes that the cult of Asclepius and his temples had been "the cradle of Greek medicine"[9] and that "Greek religious medicine crystallized around his cult."[10] Sigerist also mentions,

> "Was Hippocrates not an Asclepiad also? Was Cos, his birthplace, not the seat of the famous temple? With Hippocrates, it was said, medicine stepped out of the temples and emancipated itself from religious bonds.
>
> This seemed a logical development, but . . . today we know that rational and religious medicine did not develop one from the other but took parallel courses."[11]

For example, the introductory words to the physician's Hippocratic Oath, perhaps of Pythagorean origin, were offered as a prayer and promise to the mythical gods of health (Hygieia) and healing (Panaceia).

"I swear by Apollo Physician, and Asclepius, and Health, and Panacea and all the gods and goddesses...."[12]

Luke, The Physician

In comparison, the apostle Luke in the New Testament describes the healing powers of Jesus Christ. Jesus healed every life He touched not only in body but also in spirit and soul. In the Gospel of Luke and also in Acts, the Bible mentions 24 cases of healings by Jesus, 4 by Peter, and 6 by Paul.

The Apostle Luke, known as ... *the beloved physician* by Paul in Colossians 4:14, was a truly excellent, inspired writer and historian. As a Greek physician, he undoubtedly studied Hippocrates' theories, performing his internship in one of the temples of Asclepius. Yet, in the New Testament Luke writes only of the healing powers of the Savior, Jesus Christ. There is no mention of Asclepius healings. One example is found in Luke 5:12-13:

> *And it came to pass, when he was in a certain city, behold a man full of leprosy: who seeing Jesus fell on his face, and besought him, saying, Lord, if thou wilt, thou canst make me clean. And he put forth his hand, and touched him, saying, I will: be thou clean. And immediately the leprosy departed from him.*

Luke writes of many examples of miracles, healing, and deliverance from demonic possession:

> *And in that same hour he cured many of their infirmities and plagues, and of evil spirits; and unto many that were blind he gave sight* (Luke 7:21).

During the time Jesus Christ walked this earth revealing the true powers of God, the counterfeit of pagan, Asclepius worship experienced its peak.

Asclepius, though long dead, left behind only memories, magnified imaginations, and a desire to know only what the one, true God was able to perform. Jesus, the *great physician,* brought healing, redemption in spirit, soul, and body to everyone who received Him. As Jesus said in Matthew 9:12, . . . *They that be whole need not a physician, but they that are sick.*

This is where pagan beliefs and Christianity met with controversy and a pounding force of resentment from the Asclepius worshippers. The followers of Asclepius upheld the testimonies of his healing powers and the Christians testified of the miracles performed by Jesus Christ. The healings of Jesus Christ were even credited by some to have been the workings of Asclepius.[13]

Any miracles credited to Asclepius undoubtedly derived from Satan's counterfeit miracles as attested to by Justinus,

> ". . . and when he (sc., the devil) brings forward Asclepius as the raiser of the dead and healer of other diseases, may I say that in this matter likewise he has imitated the prophecies about Christ."[14]

With Asclepius only the pure of heart and body maintianed acceptance, but with Jesus Christ *all* who came to him received. The poor, the sickly, the rejected never were turned away or refused. Asclepius' temple home remained on this earth for his followers in this life, while Jesus Christ built an eternal home in heaven where his followers will be united with him forever. So widespread the worship of Asclepius and so prevalent the deceived followers, that Eusebius Caesariensis wrote of Asclepius as " . . . a downright destroyer, drawing them away from the true Savior and leading into godless imposture those who were susceptible to fraud . . . . "[15]

As a Greek physician, Luke does not mention the

WHERE DID THE TEMPERAMENTS ORIGINATE?

cult of Asclepius in the Scriptures (nor does he mention the temperaments). Everything Luke wrote was to glorify God through His Son, Jesus Christ. The only worldly wisdoms mentioned were in the light of leaving them behind when we come to Christ.

Jesus not only miraculously healed but proved his Lordship over the elements: feeding five thousand (John 6:10-13); walking on the water (John 6:19); feeding four thousand (Matthew 15:32); and feeding five thousand (Matthew 14:15); and calming the storm (Matthew 8:23-27). In Mark 4:41, the apostles fearfully cried out, *What manner of man is this, that even the wind and the sea obey him?*

If Asclepius did indeed exist in ancient history, his bones lay in some forgotten grave, his temples crumbled to the ground, and his memory written, not in the hearts of men, but in the records of ancient historical mythology. On the other hand, Jesus' grave is empty for he has risen; he dwells eternally within his temple residing deep within the hearts and lives of those who believe and receive Him as Lord and Savior.

Luke undoubtedly was drawn to Christianity because Jesus offered the solution for his restless wanderings and futile search for contentment. Jesus fulfilled the promise of eternal life and satisfied Luke's search for inner peace. Luke found his Savior, Jesus Christ.

4

The Development of the Four Temperaments

> "Those who rely too much on divination put too little trust in God, and the astrological practice of elections attributes to the hour what should be attributed to Jesus Christ."[1]
>
> Nicolas Oresme

Out of the ancient Greek philosophical society came the worship of Asclepius as the god of healing. As a result, the ancients incorporated idolatry into their philosophy.

The ancient Greek philosophers rejected Moses' account in the Old Testament of the origination of the universe and human beings. Philosophy became a religion comprising the beliefs of the Babylonian, Egyptian, and Persian occult practices including astrology and divination. Philosophers did not believe in one God, but theorized that a god could be anything or anyone.

The four temperaments evolved from this same philosophy of idolatry. The temperaments were the ancient philosopher's mystical interpretation of the function of the human body based upon the worship of the heavens.

Many ancient and medieval documents contain writings on the four temperaments known as the four "humours" which represent the (1) sanguine (sanguis), (2) choleric (chole), (3) melancholy (melanchole), or (4) phlegmatic (pituita). It was believed the four humours were expressed through four bodily fluids: blood, yellow bile, black bile, and phlegm.

The four bodily fluids were in turn associated with the four seasons of the year: summer, autumn, winter, and spring. The changing seasons of the year brought many festivals in celebration of the numerous Graeco-Roman deities. The theory of health and disease developed by the Hippocratic school linked the bodily humour with the temperament name and the season of the year. The following chart displays this relationship:

Humour	**Temperament**	**Season of the Year**
Yellow bile	= Choleric	= Summer
Black bile	= Melancholy	= Autumn
Phlegm	= Phlegmatic	= Winter
Blood	= Sanguine	= Spring

As Fred Lund explains in *Greek Medicine,* "The idea of black and yellow bile was arrived at by examinations of the various colors of vomitus or feces."[2] Yellow and black bile are the bitter, acidic greenish or yellow fluids secreted by the liver and assist in the body's absorption and digestion of fats. Blood is found throughout the body, while phlegm originates in the nose and mucous membranes. For example, the choleric temperament

THE DEVELOPMENT OF THE FOUR TEMPERAMENTS

would be associated with the bodily fluid yellow bile.

The Hippocratic book *On the Sacred Disease* was a treatise regarding epilepsy. According to the writer, epilepsy was really not more sacred than any other disease but rather hereditary, caused by the brain (also caused by climate—such as cold, the sun and winds), and appeared mostly in *phlegmatic* people.[3] Epilepsy was not believed to be caused by a god because a god was thought to be of the utmost purity. The author believed "The nature of all things was arranged by the gods," and "all the things take place through a divine necessity."[4] If the gods were pleased "to receive from man respect and worship" they would "repay these with favours."[5]

Hippocrates' four humours were the ancient definitions used to describe sickness, disease, the nature of the body, and also the personality type (or temperament). As an example, too much yellow or black bile may cause the brain to overheat while too much phlegm may overcool the brain causing anxiety. A healthy person was one whose four humours were in harmony. Harmony brought balance to the bodily functions.

Proper diagnosis was dependent upon identifying which humour caused the imbalance. Ancient remedies recommended rest, liquids, proper diet, herbs, and as explained in the ancient Hippocratic writings, the "Natural forces within us are the true healers of disease."[6]

The Elemental Divinities and the Temperament Theory

For medical treatment it was necessary to discover the condition and appearance of the humour, the season of the year (because people had a preponderance to certain diseases at various times of the year), and also how the humour related to the constellations (astrology) and the *elements* of nature.

As part of their cosmogony, the Greeks were originally credited with giving the name of the four elements "stichia" to their divine forces of Nature. The elements of nature were glorified as supreme deities and considered the elemental powers consisting of matter which formed the life-giving force comprising all of nature (including living and nonliving forms), the planets in heaven, and the human soul.

The elemental deities of *fire, air, earth, and water* were the gods ruling over the personality and temperaments. The temperaments were believed to be the nature of the personality which is governed by the movements of the planets in heaven (astrology). The temperaments were incorporated into this divine hierarchy. When Christians practice the temperaments they are in essence practicing the ancient philosopher's worship of the elemental deities and astrology.

The god of Air	=	Sanguine temperament
The god of Fire	=	Choleric temperament
The god of Water	=	Melancholy temperament
The god of Earth	=	Phlegmatic temperament

The Greek god Zeus represented the elemental divinity fire (choleric); Hera, air (sanguine); Aidoneus, earth (phlegmatic); and Nestis, water (melancholy). The ancient Greeks believed the heavenly planets and stars affected mankind by controlling and moving through the four elemental powers of Nature. This theory regarding the supreme forces of Nature is the basic definition of the *triplicities* of fire, air, earth, and water used in astrology. The triplicities consist of 3 fire, 3 air, 3 earth, and 3 water signs which make up the 12 signs of the astrological zodiac.

The elemental deities of fire, air, earth, and water and the practice of elemental divination evolved from this same ancient Mesopotamian culture. Geomancy (earth) divination was the practice of foretelling the future by geographical placements or by lines; aeromancy (air) was the prediction of the future by observing weather conditions or clouds and storm patterns; hydromancy (water) divination was the condition or appearance of water and how it flowed; and pyromancy (fire) divination was prediction by fire or by shapes which appeared in the flame and smoke. Astrology is the elemental divination of the heavens comprising all four of the elemental powers; it proposes that the planetary movements rule over and control the lives of countries, nations, and people on earth.

The popularity of astrology, magic, and divination in the ancient civilizations is evident in Acts 19:18-20 on Paul's missionary journey to Ephesus:

> And many that believed came, and confessed, and shewed their deeds. Many of them also which used curious arts brought their books together, and burned them before all men . . . .

Greek alchemists recognized colors as a means of identifying heavenly planets and all physical matter.[7] The four primary colors of red, white, black, and yellow were assigned to the four elements, planets, and also in the identification with bodily fluids (humour/ temperament).

Temperament	Choleric	Sanguine	Phlegmatic	Melancholy
Bodily Fluid	Yellow bile	Blood	Phlegm	Black bile
Element—Deity	Fire	Air	Earth	Water
Season	Summer	Spring	Winter	Autumn
Substance	Hot/dry	Hot/moist	Cold/dry	Cold/moist
Primary Color	Red	White	Black	Yellow

The Philosophy of Empedocles

Most testimonies regarding the temperament theory have credited Hippocrates with its conception. Actually, the Hippocratic theory of the four humours

THE DEVELOPMENT OF THE FOUR TEMPERAMENTS

was initially birthed by one of Hippocrates' predecessors named Empedocles. As stated by M.R. Wright in *Empedocles the Extant Fragment,* " . . . it was Empedocles' theory that the medical writers later took over and adapted to a fixed number of powers, and then of humours, in the body."[8] The fixed number of powers most likely represented the Greek planetary gods, astrology, and how they were thought to influence the human soul and body. In a Biblical perspective, Satan is *the prince (ruler NIV) of the power (kingdom NIV) of the air* (Ephesians 2:2). If this be so, then Satan was worshipped as a deity in his province within the elemental deity of air.

Our spiritual battle as Christians is *not aginst flesh and blood, but against principalities, against powers, against the rulers of the darkness of this world, against spiritual wickedness in high places* (Ephesians 6:12). Our physical battles are fought with spiritual weapons—the Word of God!!

A wealthy Greek poet, philosopher, physician, and priest, Empedocles was born in Acraga, Sicily around 490 B.C. (or Agrigentum, as the Romans called it). He became a much discussed and written-about person and many legends were conceived about him. He wrote two poems *On Nature* and *Purifications.* The latter describes his philosophy on the soul's passage through different life cycles (reincarnation).

Empedocles' philosophy of life centered around the ancient Graeco-Roman mythological religion which worshipped all of "Nature." He acquired his wisdom and philosophy from the ancient Egyptian and Persian civilizations. Empedocles mixed science with his mystical, philosophical religious beliefs. In today's society he would probably be a very popular "guru" type with a number of disciples following his teachings.

According to his conception of the world order, the four elemental gods were the essence of life from which all things came into being. He called these four substances "roots."[9] The elements personified divine power and character moving continually throughout the cosmos.

Empedocles became a charismatic, mystical leader. Possessing neither shyness nor humility, he considered himself to be an ancient "superman" with immortal qualities and as expressed in Helle Lambridis writings on *Empedocles,* "Hail! I wonder among you now no more a mortal but like of god immortal . . . ."[10]

Most famous for the development of his philosophy of the four elemental deities of fire, air, earth, and water, Empedocles was the first to propose that all of the elements were equally gods. His philosophy of the divinity of the four elements is clearly expressed,

> "They (elements) are for ever themselves, but running through each other they become at times different, yet are for ever and ever the same."[11]

All of the elements are bound together by two divine forces: Love and Strife. Love represented all that is "good" (strengths) and Strife was indicative of all that is "evil" (weaknesses). The temperament classifications of strengths and weaknesses evolved from Empedocles' views on astrology. When Christians study the strengths and weaknesses of each temperament type, they are studying Empedocles' doctrine on reincarnation of the soul. This is definitely not a part of Christian theology.

In attempting to understand Empedocles' conception of the world order, one may think Empedocles as an ancient comedian or accuse him of temporarily hallucinating. On his theory of the formation of mankind and the universe, he believed parts of the human anatomy and matter floated around in the air—

THE DEVELOPMENT OF THE FOUR TEMPERAMENTS

i.e., arms. heads, legs, etc.—which were separated as the result of strife in the universal order:

"... in which many a head grew without a neck, and naked arms wandered about without supporting shoulders, and eyes bereft of forehead."[12]

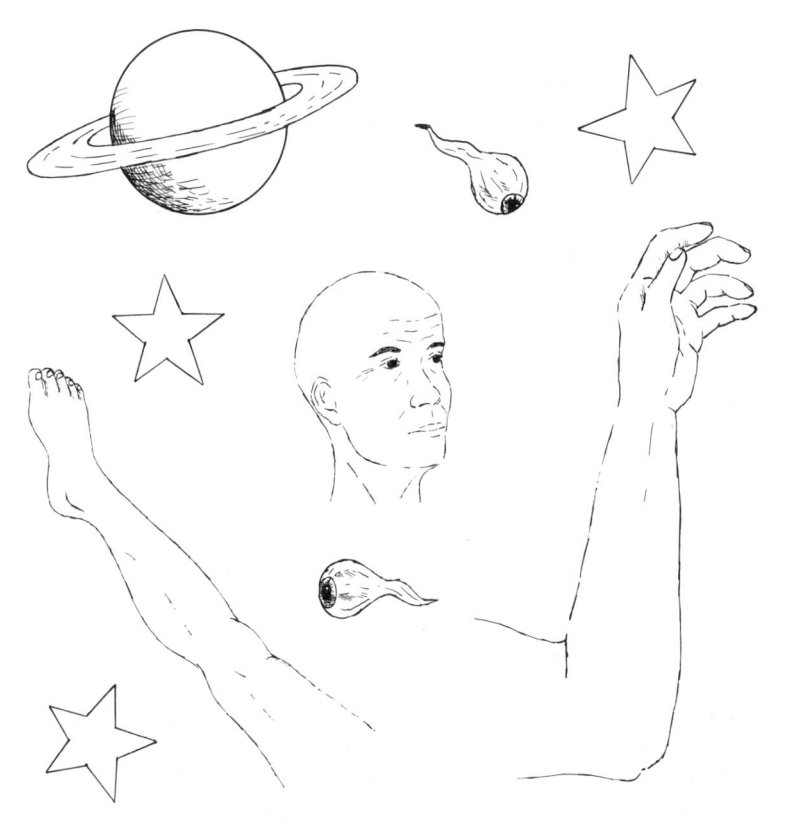

Love has a unifying affect. As a result, love joined all of these bodily parts together to form the human being and thereby brought harmony to the universe. This may be the reason so many of the ancient Graeco-Roman mythical gods and artifacts were represented as half-man and half-animal.

Empedocles' conception of the universe may have been the first to theorize the "big bang" theory which modern science still clings to. This theory is another attempt by man to eliminate any conceivable belief in the creation of the universe by Almighty God.

Empedocles' belief in reincarnation placed the soul of man in a never ending trip from one lifetime to another. He thought the immortal soul transformed at death to reinhabit animals, plants, or just about anything (metampsychosis). He himself attested to have "been a boy and a girl, and a bush and a bird and a mute fish . . . ."[13] He proposed that the souls of the obedient and wise eventually became gods, and that he himself had attained the position of immortality. To his own satisfaction, Empedocles finally reached his last incarnation making him a graduate member of the human race entitled to a place among the divinities of heaven and the full rights of immortality.

As he attested to in his writings, Empedocles' brags on his magical healing powers, raising the dead, and calming the elements. Helle Lambridis translates:

> "In the end they become seers and composers of hymns and physicians, and leaders of men on earth. From these (states) they sprout up again as gods immortal, honored above all."[14]

The legend of Empedocles indicates he committed suicide at Mount Etna in Sicily where he supposedly threw himself into a volcano. He wanted all of his disciples to see that he vanished without leaving a trace, that he had never died, and that his immortal soul passed from this world to the heavenly sphere to live eternally as a part of the celestial deity. Unfortunately, in his emotional ecstasy, he forgot his sandals at the entrance to the volcano.

An extremely driven man, Empedocles continually

searched through philosophy and religion to find the true and supreme God and the meaning of eternal life. His views were totally opposed to the Biblical account of man, creation, and the soul.

It was Empedocles who first characterized the male-female principle of opposition which is used in astrology and the temperaments. According to this principle, every male has a portion of feminine characteristics and likewise the female a certain degree of masculine characteristics (or traits). Thus, in its approach the temperament theory suggests:

Choleric	= Fire	= Hot	= Masculine
Sanguine	= Air	= Hot	= Masculine
Phlegmatic	= Earth	= Cold	= Feminine
Melancholy	= Water	= Cold	= Feminine

Combining the temperaments with the planets of astrology results in the masculine temperaments of choleric and sanguine being labeled the extrovert type of personality and the feminine phlegmatic and melancholy temperaments the introvert type.

Pythagoras—The Dramatist

Empedocles acquired his knowledge of the divine elements as a student of Pythagoras, who taught the doctrine of reincarnation (transmigration). Reincarnation theories teach that the "soul" or "psyche" is immortal and passes through many lifetimes in various forms until it reaches a state of "divinity." Reincarnation is the prevalent ideology taught in astrology.

Pythagoras combined religion with science and philosophy. He believed that all of the universe and nature was birthed through "Fire." Fire represented the supreme deity; other deities in successive order were the sun, stars, planets, moon, earth and lesser elements of air and water. He combined the microcosm (the elements of the universe in a smaller component) and the macrocosm (the entire universe in its expanse) through the study of astrology. This theory was applied to human beings and how the planets foretold their "Destiny." The human body contained the microcosm in miniature whereby the larger macrocosm of the universe controlled and manipulated the "Fate" of all human events on earth.

Pythagoras learned much of his studies of the universe from the Egyptians, Persians, and Chaldeans. According to his doctrines, the study of the universe combined with wisdom and knowledge of the mind would permit a mortal to obtain immortality. Pythagoras considered himself a prophet of the god Apollo. He taught his disciples that through a process of "purification of the mind" they, too, may some day attain an eternal position among the gods.

According to Pythagoras, the process of purification may take many lifetimes. This process occurs at death when the soul is released from its imprisonment. The soul then reincarnates into another body. The consecutive incarnations of the soul are in a higher or lower form of life depending upon the purity obtained during the previous lifetime.

A story is told where Pythagoras saw a man cruelly battering his dog. Pythagoras was emotionally distraught over the incident and pleaded with the man to release the dog. Fortunately for the dog, Pythagoras had believed it was the "soul" of a dear friend and recognized him when he heard the dog bark. Obviously, the friend of Pythagoras had not lived a previous life which qualified him to dwell in a higher life form.

If the soul reaches a complete state of purification through successive reincarnations, it then becomes an immortal god dwelling in the universe. If the lessons of purity have not been learned through successive lifetimes, then the soul is imprisoned in Hades to be eternally punished.

The theory of Pythagoras on the reincarnation of the soul is the same today as it was then. Astrology is only one example of the New Age theories which teach Pythagoras' doctrine of immortality. The doctrine of immortality through reincarnation is the predominant theme found in all of the New Age cults of today. The Bible, on the other hand, states in Hebrews 9:27, *And as it is appointed unto men once to die, but after this the judgment.*

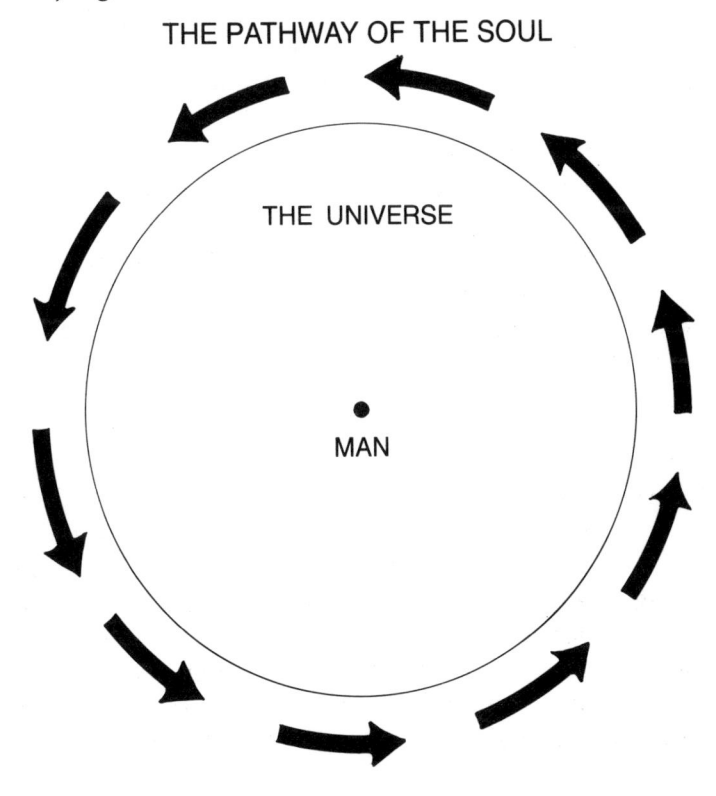

THE PATHWAY OF THE SOUL

THE UNIVERSE

MAN

TEMPERAMYSTICISM

Another Pythagorean doctrine was the concept of the circle which was a symbol of wholeness. The circle represented eternity, never-ending and continual. This was the ancient philosopher's belief in the path of the soul around the circle continually moving, stopping only for brief life-spans passing eternally through time.

Pythagoras also attributed divinity to numbers. For instance, the number "One" was the supreme god associated with eternity and "Fire." (Fire was considered the supreme god of all of the elements.) All other numbers were lesser gods. Also, "even" numbers were considered a higher deity than "odd" numbers.

Pythagoras observed the harmony between the Elements and Nature. Later, the teachings of Pythagoras and Empedocles were incorporated into the theories and practices of Hippocrates and other ancient Greek physicians. These teachings were thought to bring healing, restoration, and balance to the humours (also called bodily fluids or temperaments) through astrological interpretations.

5

The Ancient Philosopher's Religion

> Beware lest any man spoil you through philosophy and vain deceit, after the tradition of men, after the rudiments of the world, and not after Christ.
>
> Colossians 2:8

To the ancient Graeco-Roman people all of Nature was considered to be a living force. Therefore, if all things were living, they had the potential of becoming a god. Anything that was powerful or beautiful, any mystery or unexplained phenomenon, or any awe-inspiring person or circumstance may be bestowed with divine credentials.

The life-giving forces of Nature included not only higher and lower forms of life including humans, animals, and plants, but also inanimate objects such as rocks, stones, metals, the heavenly stars, planets, sun, and the moon.

TEMPERAMYSTICISM

Mythical gods and goddesses ruled and controlled every part of mankind and nature in every conceivable situation. For example, the god Robigus reigned over rust and mildew. The Romans sacrificed and worshipped in honor of Robigus in a yearly festival.

The polytheistic beliefs of the Graeco-Roman people resulted in an unlimited representation of gods and goddesses whose sanctity was jealously guarded. These ancient civilizations acquired vivid imaginations which endowed supernatural god-like powers even to human beings. An illustration of this is in Acts 14:6-18 where Paul and Barnabas preached the gospel in Lystra. When the crippled man at Lystra was healed, the people believed Paul and Barnabas to be heavenly gods who visited earth:

> ... *And when the people saw what Paul had done, they lifted up their voices, saying in the speech of Lycaonia, The gods are come down to us in the likeness of men. And they called Barnabas, Jupiter; and Paul, Mercurius, because he was the chief speaker.*

The Romans applied the name Jupiter to the god of light and the sky (also known as Zeus). He symbolized the great protector of the city and state. In astrology texts, Jupiter is credited with this same magnanimous characterization when describing the personality traits of the sign of Sagittarius as the god ruling over the people born under this sign of the zodiac. Mercurius was considered to be the god/planet Mercury which was believed to rule over the mind, speech, communication, and travel.

The priest of Jupiter wanted to sacrifice to Paul and Barnabas because the people thought the apostles were gods. Paul and Barnabas were grieved in their spirits.

THE ANCIENT PHILOSOPHER'S RELIGION

> *Which when the apostles, Barnabas and Paul, heard of, they rent their clothes, and ran in among the people, crying out, And saying, Sirs, why do ye these things? We also are men of like passions with you, and preach unto you that ye should turn from these vanities unto the living God, which made **heaven**, and **earth**, and the **sea**, and all things that are therein:*

The last verse is indicative of how the ancient Graeco-Roman civilizations devotedly worshipped their elemental deities: *heaven* (air and fire), *earth* (the earth), and the *sea* (water). Paul exhorted the people of Lystra to worship the one true God who was the creator of all things.

After the people of Lystra discovered Paul and Barnabus to be mere humans and not gods, they stoned Paul and, supposedly dead, threw him out of the city.

The fundamental principle behind this Greek theology held that superior gods gave birth to divinely lesser gods and in turn birthed mortal human beings. At death, the whole process would be reversed with certain human beings transmigrating into their former existence as deities to dwell among the heavenly stars and planets. The Greeks believed there was no beginning or ending to life. Everything that existed was birthed by something which was already in existence within the universe.

This is a direct correlation between the macrocosm (the universe without), and the microcosm (the universe within) which is exactly what astrology and other metaphysical/pseudoscience theories teach.

Persecution of the Christians

Without a doubt, the Graeco-Roman society vehemently defended and zealously worshipped their heavenly gods. Throughout ancient history, this same vehemence was demonstrated in the persecution and martyrdom of the prophets of the Old Testament and the Christians in the New Testament for their belief in the Savior, Jesus Christ.

Marcus Aurelius Antoninus born in Rome approximately A.D. 121, succeeded to the throne in 161 A.D., and reigned until his death in 180 A.D. During his reign Rome was struck with a severe plague. The panic-stricken Romans blamed their difficulties on the Christians who supposedly brought the wrath of the gods. During Aurelius' reign Christians were cruelly and inhumanly persecuted as George Long attests to in *The Meditations of Marcus Aurelius,* "the dying effort of heathenism to check the advancing tide of Christianity."[1]

This new deity represented in Christ and Christianity threatened the religious philosophies of the Graeco-Roman world and endangered the sanctity of their gods and goddesses. Christianity was thought to be a rebellious and secret sect which must be abolished to protect Rome. The Christians worshipped one God and witnessed to all people whether they were sick, poor, Roman, or Greek in an attempt to bring others into their group.

In Christianity, there was no distinction between the classes. Men, women, slaves, and free alike were all welcomed as believers. Unlike many of the Roman religions which permitted only men into their group such as Mithraism, a religious cult which celebrated its yearly festival on December 25th, and copied many of the traditions of the Christians.

Christianity was a personal insult to the Graeco-Roman world, especially the worship of one God. Christians had the audacity to refuse to join in the

THE ANCIENT PHILOSOPHER'S RELIGION

public religious worship of the Graeco-Roman deities. It was of the utmost importance to maintain good relations with their supernatural powers and for one's life to be in a harmonious relationship with the will of the gods.

Saint Alban at Verulamium was executed because he refused to worship and sacrifice to a statue of Jupiter. Also, the Greek philosopher Flavius Justinus died a martyr's death in Rome 166 A.D. after receiving Jesus Christ as Savior. He spent many years in search of the truth wading through philosophical doctrines which emptied man's intellect yet failed to fill his spiritual need. Greek philosophy did not satisfy his inner unrest for understanding the truth. At last, he found peace and a tranquil heart within the Christian faith, even in the face of death.

The result of disobedience to the gods resulted in death by martyrdom. The sacrilegious must be punished for refusing proper devotion. Disobedience was considered treachery and the ony recourse the gods would have was to send dreadful plagues and horrible circumstances upon the entire empire. This universal resentment against Christianity produced numerous martyrs throughout the first three centuries of our era.

The people of Rome were especially concerned about the Christians because they would not take part in their sacrifices, celebrations, and " . . . plainly maintained that all the heathen religions were false . . . and all the splendid ceremonies of the empire only a worship of devils.[2]

The Roman emperors unsuccessfully attempted to stop the spread of this new religion called Christianity. Finally, the only alternative left was to punish the Christians. Justin in his Apology affirms the persecution of Christians, "and that under Antoninus' rule men were put to death because they were Christians."[3]

As evidenced in Acts 19:23-35, during Paul's missionary journey the Ephesian people were quite adamant in their devotion to their goddess Diana and were outraged at the thought of abolishing her temples and statues. Demetrius earned a small fortune as a silversmith crafting silver shrines for the goddess. When he heard of Paul attempting to turn the people's hearts from the worship of the gods and fearful that this new "atheism" would spread threatening his livelihood, Demetrius started a riot among the people.

> ... So that not only this our craft is in danger to be set at nought; but also that the temple of the great goddess Diana should be despised, and her magnificence should be destroyed, whom all Asia and the world worshippeth. And when they heard these sayings, they were full of wrath, and cried out, saying, Great is Diana of the Ephesians. And the whole city was filled with confusion.... Some therefore cried one thing, and some another ... and all with one voice about the space of two hours cried out, Great is Diana of the Ephesians. And when the townclerk had appeased the people, he said, Ye men of Ephesus, what man is there that knoweth not how that the city of the Ephesians is a worshipper of the great goddess Diana, and of the image which fell down from Jupiter?

For all of the pagan Graeco-Roman society, this Biblical reference demonstrates the common theological theme of the Graeco-Roman world, their interpretation of the cosmic heavens, and their belief in the elemental powers.

In his poem on *Meditations,* Marcus Aurelius speaks of the Greek philosophy on the immortality of the soul and its connection to the elemental powers.

> ". . . so the souls which are removed into the air after subsisting for some time are transmuted and diffused, and assume a fiery nature by being received into the seminal intelligence of the universe, and in this way make room for the fresh souls which come to dwell there . . . and the transformations into the aerial or the fiery element."[4]

6
Astrology Among The Graeco-Roman Civilizations

"My Bible tells me how to go to heaven,
not how the heavens go."[1]

J.R. Cohu

The Cosmogony of the Ancient Philosophers

Beneath the moon were the zones of the four Elemental deities of fire, air, water, and earth followed by persons, animals, and objects. The four elemental deities and the planetary constellations were given tremendous powers, especially the element of air. Air was the haven for friendly and vicious demonic powers dwelling in the heavenly sphere separating the celestial deities from human beings and lower life-forms.

TEMPERAMYSTICISM

Ancient astrology became more than an astral religion under the Graeco-Roman civilizations. In speaking of the religion of Greece, Andre-Jean Festugiere in *Personal Religion Among the Greeks* notes, " . . . the religion of the Cosmic God, or of the Cosmos as a god, or even of the stars, was the current form of personal religion . . . ."[2]

The sun, moon, and five planets (Saturn, Jupiter, Mars, Venus, and Mercury) were considered not only divine, but also the instruments controlling destiny. Accepted as divine heirarchy, the planetary configurations maintained the position of the immutable, fixed powers influencing and affecting all of life on earth.

In the heavens resided the home of the ancients' cosmic deities. Each deity was assigned a planetary kingdom from which to rule and reign above the lowly mortal's temporal, earthly environment below. Lynn Thorndike in the *The History of Magic and Experimental Science* states,

> "Some ancient philosophers held that by intense imagination the souls of men could be united to the Intelligence of the moon, which, they said, ruled the four elements and everything from the sphere of the moon to the center of the earth."[3]

The Graeco-Roman astrologers fine-tuned their skills by studying ancient Babylonian scrolls. These ancient astrologers were the learned and called the *mathematici*. They acquired "the learning" from ancient Babylonian and Chaldean priests. The *mathematici*, in time, became quite skilled in the extremely complicated practice of constructing horoscopes. The complexity of astrology with its minute details intentionally afforded a way of escape should the prediction be erroneous due to some obscure detail which had been overlooked. In this way, the astrologers hailed the accuracy of their predictions while excusing mistakes as a miscalculation and not representative of errors in the heavens.

Astrology and Ancient Medicine

The religions of Babylon and Egypt influenced Graeco-Roman medicine and much of their scientific methods reflected the Babylonian culture especially in the practice of divination and astrology. Many of the ancient drugs, surgical instruments, and medical practices were derived from Egypt. The Egyptians worshipped the healing god/physician Imhotep, while the Greeks deified their healing god/physician Aeclepius. The Graeco-Roman civilizations converted religion into their own philosophical perception of science and medicine.

Mankind's physical nature was thought to be comprised of the four elemental deities (humours) which in turn were controlled by the movement of the planetary constellations.

Astrology became a significant tool in the diagnosis and treatment of disease maintaining the knowledge of the planetary positions as a prerequisite to the study of all bodily functions. Manly Palmer Hall in *The Story of Astrology* attests to the fact that "Astrology from the time of Hippocrates, was regarded as an extremely valuable aid in the diagnosing of disease . . . ."[4]

Planets (Graeco-Roman gods) ruled over bodily functions, and the planetary positions (favorable or unfavorable emotions of the gods) determined health or disease. An individual's destiny remained under the influence (positive or negative) of the planetary configurations. According to the early physicians, planetary positions precisely calculated revealed a specific disease and also determined the appropriate remedy.

Galen (Claudius Galenus): A Man of the Temperaments

Several of the Christian temperament books have credited the works of Galen as an important contributor to the temperament philosophy. What does history say about Galen?

Claudius Galenus (Galen) was born approximately 129 A.D. in Pergamos in Greece. As both philosopher and physician, Galen exerted a powerful influence during the Middle Ages. At this time the study of the planetary positions contributed extensively to the classification of disease and its treatment.

Galen was deeply influenced by the work of Cladius Ptolemy, one of the foremost astrologer-mathemeticians of his time period (approximately 127-151 A.D.). Ptolemy's work, *Tetrabiblos* (approximately 140 A.D.) was an astrological exposition on the stars and their influence on humanity.

Galen's prolific writing abilities included over 400 books. Many of his theories incorporated the fundamentals of treatment through both astrological medicine and also on the basis of experience. His treatise *Prognostication of Disease* explains certain days when the position of the moon indicates a tendency toward disease; from this prognostication he prescribes the appropriate treatment.

In his writings, Galen expressed belief in omens, superstitions, magic and astrology including his devoted interest in the manuscripts of ancient astrological writings. Most noted for his works on anatomy, physiology, and surgery, Galen's literary treatises were based on his experience as the physician

ASTROLOGY AMONG THE GRAECO-ROMAN CIVILIZATIONS

to the gladiators and the Emperor Marcus Aurelius (who murdered and persecuted Christians).

A great sanctuary was built and dedicated to the god Asclepius in Pergamon where Galen practiced medicine. Throughout his life Galen strictly followed the cult of Asclepius and devotedly worshipped Asclepius as his god.

As a Stoic philosopher, Galen's religion was of the "mind, based on the results of philosophical inquiry."[5] Galen's views consisted of one universal religion which deified "the mind and intellect." He thought Christians invented stories describing eternal life with the Lord.[6] Philosophy and the mind were considered the pathway to the gods and "it has become the duty of the philosopher to interpret the new outlook to mankind."[7] He rejected Moses' biblical account of the story of creation, claiming that it was unscientific.[8] Moses was considered to be just like any other philosopher and his account of the creation in Genesis considered antiquated and therefore rejected.

Galen outwardly tolerated, but inwardly disliked, the Jews and Christians. He believed the reliance of the Old Testament prophets' and the present day Christians' on faith in the one true God should be substituted by logic, reasoning, and philosophy.[9] As a student of the stars, Galen's philosophy held "divine wisdom could be equally discovered in the microcosm of the animal and in the universe as a whole."[10]

Eusebius, an author in the early third century, in speaking of the stars, wrote a letter to Theodotus, the tanner explaining the futile pursuit of astrology, " . . . Deserting the Holy Scriptures of God they pursue the study of geometry since they are of the earth and their talk is of the earth and they know not Him that comes from above."[11]

Galen contributed philosophical thought and theory to modern medicine; yet, he was anti-Christ in his belief in God. Sadly, he believed there would be hope for the Chrisitians if they would turn to logic, philosophy, or even his own theories of reasoning.[12]

The views of these ancient Greek philosophers are very similar to the doctrines of the New Age cults which appeal to "the mind as god." History does repeat itself!

According to the *Biographical Dictionary of Psychology*, Galen accepted the animal spirit doctrine of his ancestors especially Erasistratus. Galen connected the four ventricles of the brain to the control and direction of animal spirits. These animal spirits, operating through the nerves, caused the muscles to move.[13]

Also, the *Biographical Dictionary of Psychology* indicates Galen took from Hippocrates the association established by the four elements of Empedocles and the four bodily humors. Galen then developed it into the four-fold typology of the sanguine, melancholic, choleric, and phlegmatic temperaments.[14]

In comparing the superiority of man to plants Galen, *On the Parts of the Body*, expresses his opinion on the composition of the human body (the temperaments) and the intelligence of the heavenly planets. The planets are spoken of as if they were personified beings superior in intelligence to humans.

> "When a surpassing intelligence comes into being in such slime—for what else would one call a thing composed of fleshes, blood, phlegm, and yellow and black bile?—how great we must consider the pre-eminence of the intelligence in the sun, moon and stars?"[15]

Saint Hildegard

Hildegard, born approximately 1098 A.D. on the River Nahe near Sponheim, was considered by many of her time a prophetess and visionary. She spent most of her life in religious monastaries due to her frequent illnesses. Her frequent sick spells, possibly a nervous disorder, were plagued by trances and visions which she attributed to God.

These supernatural visions, for the most part, contained a blinding or bright light which she interpreted with spiritual significance crediting these visions to inspiration from God.

Hildegard was most renowned for her involvement in the elements, temperaments, medicine, and for her prognostications. She combined a mystical use of the four temperaments with her visions, astrology and the Bible. Hildegard was recommended for sainthood but never officially cannonized by the pope.

Hildegard used magic and superstition for healing. As explained in Lynn Thorndike's *History of Magic and Experimental Science*, Hildegard condemned magic and then offered recommendations to counteract evil spells with astrology, herbs, animal parts, incantations and ceremonies.[16]

Hildegard can be credited with the expansion of the four temperaments and astrology into modern theology. She received much of her inspiration from the mystical writer Hugh of Saxony (1096-1141). Many of her philosophical teachings on the temperaments were combined with Biblical doctrines which have traveled throughout history to this present day.

In Hildegard's writings, she included Empedocles' conception of the four elements, the humors, and nature. She also taught on the relationship between the macrocosm and the microcosm. She wrote

TEMPERAMYSTICISM

extensively about the spiritual significance of the four seasons, solstices and equinoxes, and the parallel between the four elements and the four cardinal points (north, south, east, and west).

In "Causae et curae" she assumed, ". . . various types of men are delineated according to the combinations of humours in their bodies, and their characters are sketched and even their fate to some extent predicted therefrom."[17]

"In the case of choleric, sanguine, melancholy, and phlegmatic men, Hildegard states what the relations of each type will be with women and even to some extent what sort of children they will have."[18] Hildegard claimed that through astrological predictions she could interpret death, birth of a male or female child, and illness. Also, she believed the planets were associated with the human anatomy, the head being the sun, the moon and stars to the eyes, etc. As an example, Hildegard believed, "the moon simply affects the air, and the air affects man's blood and the humors of the body."[19]

From Hildegard's perception the temperaments grew into a full-fledged theological principle ihtermixing mysticism with the Bible. Her theories passed from theologians to ancient physicians to alchemists and were not revived until the early 1900's.

One of the first books to have been written on the temperaments within the last thirty years and associated with the Bible is O. Hallesby's, *Temperament and the Christian Faith*, Augsburg Publishing House, Minneapolis, Minnesota, 1962, upon which many of the current temperament enthusiasts have acquired their inspiration.

Dr. Hallesby, a professor at the Independent Theological Seminary, died in Norway on November

22, 1961. Although he only visited America once in his lifetime, he exerted a powerful influence on the Lutheran church.

Dr. Hallesby gives a precautionary explanation in his book: "The temperaments are imaginary quantities. They are certainly never found in life just as we describe them here."[20] He goes on to say, "Every person constitutes some sort of mixture of temperaments; and no one individual could serve as an example of a single, 'pure' temperament."[21]

I believe Dr. Hallesby's writings have the scattered flavoring of Hildegard. As with Hildegard, Dr. Hallesby believed the temperaments were created for God's kingdom. This is very similar to the customary Medieval interpretation of mysticism and religion.

One would think that if the temperament theory, being such a prominent teaching in the Christian church, was created from scripture or connected in some way to scripture, there would be some Biblical references to it.

7
The Temperaments, Astrology, and Medicine

And mine hand shall be upon the prophets that see vanity, and that divine lies: they shall not be in the assembly of my people, neither shall they be written in the writing of the house of Israel, neither shall they enter into the land of Israel; and ye shall know that I am the Lord God.
                                               Ezekiel 13:9

The Medical Horoscope
Ancient physicians constructed an individual's astrology chart, called a horoscope, at the onset of an illness. The astrologer/physician would determine from the chart whether the patient would live or die, and also to determine a prescribed treatment.

TEMPERAMYSTICISM

Temperament Type	Astrology Sign	Ruling God/Planet
Choleric	Leo	Sun
	Sagittarius	Jupiter
	Aries	Mars
Sanguine	Gemini	Mercury
	Libra	Venus
	Aquarius	Uranus
Phlegmatic	Taurus	Venus
	Virgo	Mercury
	Capricorn	Saturn
Melancholy	Pisces	Neptune
	Cancer	Moon
	Scorpio	Pluto

THE TEMPERAMENTS, ASTROLOGY, AND MEDICINE

Bodily Humour	Elemental Deity	Bodily Function
Yellow Bile	Fire	Heart, Spine Back
		Thighs, Liver Hips
		Head, Sex Glands
Blood	Air	Nerves, Arms Shoulders, Brain
		Kidneys
		Blood Circulation
Phlegm	Earth	Throat, Neck Intestines
		Nervous System Brain
		Knees, Bones Skin, Teeth
Black Bile	Water	Feet
		Stomach, Digestion Breast, Liver
		Sex Organs

According to astrological beliefs, a person's destiny, favorable or unfavorable, is based upon the positions of the planets at birth. To determine where the planets were located, the ancient astrologers used an *ephemeris* showing the planetary positions on the particular day and month of the year at the moment of birth. The planetary positions were placed within the horoscope to explain the person's personality, temperament, future, and health.

In medical astrology, the Sun as a god ruled over the heart, while Jupiter ruled over the liver, Saturn the bones, Mercury the brain, the Moon over digestion and other internal organs, and Mars the sex glands. The patient's horoscope became the tool used by the astrologer/physician to aid in the diagnosis and treatment of the illness. The ancient's believed illness resulted from negative influences of the planetary positions within the patient's horoscope.

For example, before being discovered and named as a planet in 1781 by William Herschel (1738-1822), Uranus (also known as Zeus to the Greeks and Jupiter to the Romans) was the appointed "god of the sky." Uranus and Gaea, "the god of the earth," were the parents of the Titans—the first mythological race.

The astrologer/physician constructed a horoscope for an individual with a blood (sanguine) disorder ("bleeding" the patient was quite common in ancient and medieval medical practices). Uranus is the ruling planet (a god) over the astrology sign of Aquarius. Aquarius is a *sanguine* sign ruling over the blood (sanguine temperament) and circulatory system. The symbol for Uranus is then placed in the horoscope to determine if it is in a positive (strengths) or negative (weaknesses) relationship of one planet to another. The god/planet, astrology sign, and aspect determined the cause and remedy for the illness.

The sanguine temperament is comprised of the following interrelationships: Uranus represents the ruling god over the sign Aquarius. Aquarius is the divine element Air. Uranus and Aquarius rule over the bodily humour blood. Uranus, Aquarius, the bodily humour of blood, and the elemental deity of air equally comprise the sanguine temperament.

Sanguine Temperament

Uranus	=	a god/planet
	(rules over)	
Aquarius	=	astrology sign
	(rules over)	
Blood	=	bodily humor
	(rules over)	
Air	=	elemental deity

The final step was to determine whether the planet was in a fortunate or unfortunate relationship with other "aspects" of the patient's horoscope. From the patient's horoscope, physicians would determine (1) which god/planet ruled over the patient's anatomy, and (2) which procedures to use for a possible cure, or (3) whether the patient would live or die.

The Hippocratic theory of the temperaments is in actuality an interpretation of the elemental deities of fire, air, earth, and water worshipped in the ancient Graeco-Roman civilizations. These elements combined with astrology translate into the temperaments and transferred from the predecessors of Pythagoras and then to Empedocles, Hippocrates, Plato, Aristotle, Galen, and down through history.

> "The Arabs developed and extended this theory, describing the sanguine, phlegmatic, and choleric constitutional types.... Combined with astrological elements the theory was developed and extended still further in the West in the Middle Ages and Renaissance."[1]

John of Rupescissa was a Franciscan born approximately 1300 A.D. He was a medieval prophet, alchemist, and astrologer/physician who believed, "Ierapigra draws humours from the head, neck, and breast, but not from the lower members because it is governed by the stars of Aries, Taurus, and Gemini which control those parts of the body."[2] He thought melancholy persons were those temperaments influenced by the negative influences and nature of the slow-moving planet Saturn.[3] Ancient/medieval medicine associated sluggish behavior to the planet Saturn and its influence affecting the melancholy temperament.

Antonio of Cartagena in 1530 wrote a treatise on critical days regarding certain poisons and the cure of fevers. The influence of the stars and demon spirits affected certain temperament types. "The persons most apt to receive this power from the stars are old melancholic or hot choleric temperaments while children of a moist and tender constitution are the most readily affected."[4]

Ancient/medieval medicine incorporated the practice of astrology and magic up to the Seventeenth Century. William of Conches (born 1133) prepared several treatises including writings on demons, magic, astrology and astronomy. His theories based on the temperaments and the four divine elements (fire, air,

THE TEMPERAMENTS, ASTROLOGY, AND MEDICINE

earth, and water) were thought to comprise all of earth, man, and animals.

> "Of land animals choleric ones, like the lion, possess most fire; phlegmatic ones, like pigs, most water; and melancholic ones, like the cow and ass, most earth."[5]

Conches' theory of the temperaments illustrates how profoundly the elemental deities and temperaments contributed to the philosophies of ancient civilizations throughout medieval history and medicine. Conches writings implied the planets in heaven and the four elements controlled the physical nature of the human body.

Even throughout the Seventeenth Century much of the doctrine of the four humours was combined with astrological principles in medicine. As Lynn Thorndike explains, "Humoral considerations, however, dominate Hippocratic medicine even in writing where this is not stated explicitly . . . ."[6] In regards to the unscientific philosophy of the four humours of the body, John Maxson Stillman explains in his book, *Theophrastus Bombastus Von Hohenheim, Called Paracelsus* that this theory,

> . . . "had become complicated with astrology and other mysticisms, while the superstitutions of the medieval Church, and the heathen superstitions of the northern European peoples were not without their influence upon local medicinal practice."[7]

Many of the ancient/medieval physicians and theologians practiced this mixture of the occult and the Bible. Any study of history would reveal this corrupt interpretation of God's word; yet, amidst the many were those few who stood true.

TEMPERAMYSTICISM

William of Auvergne wrote in *De legibus* that he "condemned astrology, and observing the elements because this was idolatry."[8]

8
The Philosophy of the Soul

> The intellect of man sits visibly enthroned upon his forehead and in his eye, and the heart of man is written upon his countenance. But the soul reveals itself in the voice only, as God revealed Himself to the prophet of old in the still small voice, and in the voice from the burning bush.[1]
>
> Henry Wadsworth Longfellow

The concept of the temperament theory in its Christianized "New Age" format is a listing of *Strengths* and *Weaknesses* associated with each temperament type. The strengths and weaknesses listed with each of the temperament types are in actuality the conception of Empedocles' doctrine of "Love" (Philia) versus "Strife" (Neikos) and associated with the ancients' moral principles of "good" versus "evil."

This concept of good and evil appeared in the ancient astrologers' use of the *circle* or *sphere* representing a belief that at death the divine soul travels into a cyclic transference which manifests itself in another life form (reincarnation). The circle represents infinity, having no beginning or ending. Pythagoras believed "God is a circle whose center is everywhere and whose circumference is nowhere."[2]

The strengths indicative of the higher evolved soul and were linked to the divinities of Nature. The concept of evil was based on the wicked and corrupt works performed by the "soulish" nature during one's lifetime.

In ancient Greece the soul lived as the fiery breath of life. The soul was believed to be the lightest of the four elements of air, fire, water, and earth. Being lighter than the substance of the heavier elements, the soul naturally would rise above the heavy, dense atmosphere of the earth.

The "good soul" at death departed, ascending to the heavenly planets and stars. The soul remained in its heavenly abode until it descended to inhabit another life; or, if the soul reached a state of perfection (or purity) during its earthly life, it remained in heaven to dwell as a tribute to immortality. The "evil soul" would be confined, imprisoned on the earth to wander the earth's surface living among the demons or be sent to Hades for eternal punishment.

The lesson in this example of the immortality of the soul is simply: If a person tried hard enough, lived righteously enough, never angered the gods (intentionally or unintentionally), and lived a life worthy of honor, they have purified the soul, thereby granting them permission to become a divine being.

THE PHILOSOPHY OF THE SOUL

Probably the most important aspect of obtaining immortality and eternal security was in pleasing the gods. If a god intentionally or unintentionally became offended, one must submit to a "purification" process usually involving water and animal sacrifice. Water washed and cleansed away the act of disobedience, and then as a sign of repentence blood sacrifice finally appeased the gods. The process of water cleansing by the pagans is the counterfeit to the Christian's baptism by water.

One of the most profound examples of good versus evil is found in Genesis 3:5. Satan's strategy for Eve was to obtain forbidden knowledge, the desire for self-exaltation and the temptation of God-likeness. *For God doth know that in the day ye eat thereof, then your eyes shall be opened, and ye shall be as gods, knowing good and evil.*

This is the deception perpetrated by Satan of reversing evil for good *and good evil; that put darkness for light, and light for darkness* (Isaiah 5:20) and is held in the ancient philosophers' concept of the soul—the exaltation of self. Within Greek philosophy the eternal, omnipotent Jehovah God was left outside of, and separated from, His creation. Ancient Greek philosophy placed man in the position as "god" and defined nature as the "divine force." Mortal human beings rejecting God; rejecting the truth, and choosing a lie. Not unlike today's "New Age" philosophy, the mind (soul or psyche) is thought to be the way to salvation and in its expression "any just and perfect being is god."

Paul's missionary journey to Athens (approximately 53 A.D.) details his confrontation with Greek philosophers (Acts 17:18-21). The Bible says of Paul, . . . *his spirit was stirred in him* . . . . when he saw the city of Athens given over to total idolatry.

TEMPERAMYSTICISM

> *Then certain philosophers of the Epicureans, and of the Stoicks, encountered him. And some said, What will this babbler say? other some, He seemeth to be a setter forth of strange gods: because he preached unto them Jesus, and the resurrection. And they took him, and brought him unto Areopagus, saying, May we know what this new doctrine, whereof thou speakest is? For thou bringest certain strange things to our ears: we would know therefore what these things mean. (For all the Athenians and strangers which were there spent their time in nothing else, but either to tell, or to hear some new things.)*

The Greek philosophers intensely curious about new deities or unusual philosophies contradictory to their own understanding, would either adopt or totally reject these new gods solely based upon philosophy. If they welcomed the new additions to their hierarchy, considerable energy would be given in an attempt to understand the deeper philosophical meanings represented by these gods so they could be equally worshipped with other deities.

Not satisfied for the representations of gods and goddesses (carved from gold, silver, stone or wood) to remain in the temples or sanctuaries, the ancients placed them throughout the streets of the Graeco-Roman world. Idols and statues with favorite deities were placed everywhere in the cities so that when one passed they might offer prayers at any time during the day or night.

The Graeco-Roman religion worshipped, sacrificed, in supplication and obedience to their numerous divinities. The ancient philosophers even offered their deities a counterfeit prayer similar to the New Testament's John 1:1.

THE PHILOSOPHY OF THE SOUL

> "First origin of my origin, first beginning of my beginning, breath of breath, first of the breath that is in me, fire, god-given for my blending of the blendings in me, first of the fire in me, water of water, first of the water in me, earthly substance, first of the earthly substance in me, perfect body of me."[3]

This prayer was the philosophical invocation to the cosmic god of the four elements. It was the worship of the outer world of the divinities which were blended together and miniaturized in the human body. This philosophical theory intimately connecting the heavens to a cosmic god resulted in the ancient's belief in the divinity of the human soul.

Paul's sermon on Mars' Hill in Athens (Acts 17:22-32) depicts not only his cautious approach to the people but also the Athenians' ardent devotion and commitment to their gods when Paul reveals the one true God. Most rejected Paul's words, some wanted to hear more, but only a handful made a decision to follow Christ that day. Paul warned them to repent and to stop ignorantly clinging to spiritually worthless idols made by man.

> *Then Paul stood in the midst of Mars' hill and said, Ye men of Athens, I perceive that in all things ye are too superstitious. For as I passed by, and beheld your devotions, I found an altar with this inscription,* **to the unknown god,** *Whom therefore ye ignorantly worship, him declare I unto you. God that made the world and all things therein, seeing that he is Lord of heaven and earth, dwelleth not in temples made with hands; Neither is worshipped with men's hands, as though he needed any thing, seeing he giveth to all life, and breath, and all things.*

According to ancient pagan beliefs the way to become a god and immortality could be obtained basically in living the present life as a "good," obedient person and not offending the gods. Because of their high-standing in society, Empedocles believed the physician and prophet had reached their final incarnation and now attained the position of immortality as a god. This probably accounted for Empedocles' exalted view of himself.

The doctrine of the reincarnated soul nature represented an attempt by man to gain salvation and eternal security through earthly *works*. However, the Bible says salvation and eternal life cannot be obtained through goodness or good works. *For all have sinned and come short of the glory of God* (Romans 3:23). As Ephesians 2:8-9 states: *For by grace are ye saved through faith; and that not of yourselves: it is the gift of God: Not of works, lest any man should boast.* We are saved not by our works, but rather through faith in Jesus Christ.

9

Temperaments or TemperaMysticism

For the word of God is quick, and powerful, and sharper than any two-edged sword, piercing even to the dividing asunder of soul and spirit, and of the joints and marrow, and is a discerner of the thoughts and intents of the heart.

Hebrews 4:12

Good or Evil—Strengths or Weaknesses?

The temperament philosophy proposes that an individual's personality is expressed through one or more of the combinations of temperament types. To demonstrate the astrology/temperament connection, the following "illustrative" list consists of the strengths and weaknesses of each temperament type *according to their astrological element of air, fire, water, and earth.* These terms represent the same personality profile

Strengths

Sanguine	Choleric	Melancholy	Phlegmatic
Charming	Strength	Dependable	Conservative
Sincere	Determined	Diligent	Stable
Intuitive	Quick	Responsible	Practical
Cheerful	Bold	Emotional	Adaptable
Talkative	Adventurous	Deep	Temperance
Communicative	Enthusiastic	Intuitive	Practical
Imaginative	Assertive	Sensitive	Persistance
Graceous	Energetic	Disciplined	Resourceful
Compassionate	Driven	Loyal	Dependable
Lively	Confident	Tenacious	Thorough
Direct	Decisive	Idealistic	Kindness
Easy-going	Direct	Determined	Responsible
Witty	Active	Maternal-instinct	Modest
Independent	Sports-lover	Protective	Cautious
Extrovert	Extrovert	Introvert	Introvert

Weaknesses

Sanguine	Choleric	Melancholy	Phlegmatic
Changeable	Domineering	Calculating	Slowness
Restless	Impatient	Moody	Lazy
Fickle	Manipulating	Pessimistic	Detached
Unstable	Selfish	Temperamental	Controlling
Unreliable	Cold	Suspicious	Stubborn
Undisciplined	Combative	Dogmatic	Fearful
Aloof	Violent	Unforgiving	Doubtful
Naive	Critical	Indecision	Negativity
Feelings of inferiority	Rebellious	Proud	Anxious
Overly sensitive	Egotist	Worrier	Procrastinate
Inconsistent	Aggressive	Cruel	Worrier
Rebellious	Rude	Sadistic	Finicky
Unpredictable	Sarcastic	Narrow-minded	Excessively dependent

descriptions I used in astrology. After you read this list you may want to compare it with the terms used in temperament books. As you will see, this same comparative terminology of strengths and weaknesses found in Christian-authored temperament books are the same general descriptions of zodiac signs found in astrology texts.

Astrology birthed the elemental deities and the elemental deities birthed the temperament theory.

Most likely at this point, temperament teachers would label the author as a critically bold choleric or perhaps a gloom-and-doom melancholy. Then again there are very good indications the author could be a phlegmatic or a truth-seeking, adventurous sanguine.

Generally, depending upon our moods and feelings at any moment, any combination of the temperament classifications of weaknesses and strengths could be applied to our personality or emotional situation.

Actually, I was born under the astrology sign of Aquarius which classifies me in the category of the sanguine temperament type. Then there is a slight blending of Leo and Capricorn which means I am a little bit choleric and a dash of phlegmatic.

Truthfully, it is much more spiritually edifying to be considered "a new creation," because the old nature is gone. It is no longer necessary for me to classify myself according to the doctrines of astrology.

Tim LaHaye explains this "new creation" passage in his book, *Spirit-Controlled Temperament* (Tyndale House Publishers, Inc., 1966 Illinois, pg. 8) quoting Paul in II Corinthians 5:17:

> *Therefore if any man be in Christ, he is a new creature: old things are passed away; behold, all things are become new.*

In this context, Tim LaHaye explains his teaching on

the temperaments based upon strengths and weaknesses. As we found earlier, the temperament strengths and weaknesses originated with the philosopher Empedocles.

The weaknesses in temperament appears to be part of the natural man (old nature) and the strengths the divine (new) nature of Jesus Christ. He cites the Apostle Peter as an example stating, ". . . his temperament was vastly changed by receiving the 'new nature' "(Pg. 8). Here again, if we apply the strengths and weaknesses of the temperament theory to scripture, we are adding ancient philosophical doctrines to the truths of the Bible.

Is Paul speaking of the fleshly man as a new creation or the spiritual man? I believe Paul answered this question in II Corinthians 5:16 when he professed that:

> . . . know we no man after the flesh: yea, though we have known Christ after the flesh, yet now henceforth know we him no more.

Clearly Paul was speaking of the spiritual man. When we are born-again it is the "spiritual" nature which is a "new creation." Our old, dead spirit is quickened, now alive by the power of the Holy Spirit.

> Now we have received, not the spirit of the world, but the spirit which is of God . . . (I Corinthians 2:12).

The divine nature of Jesus Christ resides within our fleshly bodies.

> Know ye not that ye are the temple of God, and that the Spirit of God dwelleth in you?
> (I Corinthians 3:16)

Spiritual things are revealed and taught to us by the Holy Spirit.

> Which things also we speak, not in the words which man's wisdom teacheth, but which the Holy

TEMPERAMYSTICISM

Ghost teacheth; comparing spiritual things with spiritual (I Corinthians 2:13).

Jesus Christ's divine nature dwelling within the body of a believer is in no way related to the strengths and weaknesses of the ancient philosophers' concept of the four temperament theory of the personality.

But the natural man receiveth not the things of the Spirit of God: for they are foolishness unto him: neither can he know them, because they are spritually discerned (I Corinthians 2:14).

When you compare the different personality theories emerging within the Christian community, notice that all of these systems intermix the Fruit of the Spirit, strengths and weaknesses, and how—by applying their system's principles—one might overcome weaknesses to obtain godlikeness (strengths). This is all very subtley interwoven with scripture. In later chapters, I will explain these comparisons.

Personally, rather than empasizing the power of the temperaments, Tim LaHaye, Florence Littauer, and others should have limited their focus to the transforming power of the Holy Spirit—leaving the temperaments out completely. It is difficult, if not impossible, to endorse the temperament teaching in any relationship to the Bible.

Temperament Type and Astrology

Both the temperament theory and astrology explain that an individual's personality is expressed through a combination of one or more of these temperament traits. The expression of the temperaments is identical to the expression of the sun-sign in astrology; both represent the ego or the personality of the person. For example, a typical sanguine might be 40% phlegmatic

TEMPERAMENTS OR TEMPERAMYSTICISM

but 60% sanguine; or, a combination of a third temperament trait added to the other two.

In astrology, the zodiac sign of Capricorn (a person born December 13 through January 19) is also considered an earth sign. The personality of a Capricorn would be expressed predominantly as the phlegmatic temperament type. Like the temperament descriptions, astrology also combines more than one personality trait to describe the personality.

For example, a Capricorn (earth sign/phlegmatic temperament) with the planetary position of the moon placed in the zodiac under Aquarius (air sign/sanguine temperament), would be considered a combination of the phlegmatic/sanguine temperament. In successive order the astrologer would completely follow through the planetary configurations and "aspects" to derive their prognostications of the personality type, and then proceed to foretell that person's destiny by reading their astrology chart. The temperaments were used by the ancient astrologers as the simplistic first step in a process to determine the overall personality description used by the practicing astrologer.

The temperament teachers explain how to have harmonious relationships with a spouse, children, and friends by knowing temperament types. In addition to relationships, the temperament enthusiasts claim careers or professional occupations best suited for a particular temperament type. Astrology claims these same categorizations of people according to their horoscope.

The temperament enthusiasts even unknowingly associate these astrological terms as a part of Christian service. By using Galatians 5:22-23 they incorporate the temperaments into the Word of God. This is an attempt to convince others that the temperament theory is a valid part of a Christian's spiritual life. The pagan, idolatrous religion of astrology is not the Gospel of Jesus Christ and astrology cannot be sanctified because it is blended with scriptures.

Both the temperaments and astrology have simplified the entire complex nature of the personality and assembled it into a four-walled impenetrable structure of the personality, calling in the temperaments. This implies that the personality can only move in four

TEMPERAMENTS OR TEMPERAMYSTICISM

directions (or at the most 12) which are preprogrammed descriptions of the personality.

This short-sighted view of the personality is similar to a huge checker board with humans as the playing pieces. The king moves in one direction and the knight another. The rules say you cannot move in any direction other than the one already designated.

It would be so much more liberating to think of the personality as a beautiful multi-faceted diamond, each one different from another in shape, size, and color. Before viewing it in its final state at your local jewelry store, the diamond for hundreds of years was being *formed* beneath the earth's crust and *shaped* by heat and pressure. This extreme heat forced the diamond to crystallize ultimately to become a valuable, transparent stone.

The personality, like the diamond, is shaped and formed throughout life by environment, heredity, acquired habits, attitudes, and reactions. The power to change the personality comes from God.

It's the self-life (ego) which produces the "I" syndrome: selfish, demanding, and unkind. God wants to mold Christian's lives through the softening process of the Holy Spirit which results in love, gentleness, maturity, and in a selfless life. Becoming the person God wants us to be brings the greatest personal satisfaction and the highest fulfillment in life.

Personality Theories

The study of personality theories is as old as recorded history. Even though personality studies are not new, there has been a renewal of ancient personality theories which have their origins in Eastern mysticism, witchcraft, astrology, and the occult.

Today's society, more than every before, is intrigued by the many facets of the personality. Discontentment with personal shortcomings releases a rush of humanistic and transpersonal psychological theories to offer answers to the puzzling questions regarding "the self." There is an innate curiosity in searching the depths of the inner soul to discover the true person within and then answer the all-encompassing question, "Why do I act the way I do?"

The Bible and The Personality

"The self" is the soul operating through the personality. According to God's Word, man is spirit, soul, and body.

> *And the very God of peace sanctify you wholly; and I pray God your whole spirit and soul and body be preserved blameless unto the coming of our Lord Jesus Christ* (I Thessalonians 5:23).

> *And the Lord God formed man of the dust of the ground, and breathed into his nostrils the breath of life; and man became a living soul* (Genesis 2:7).

Adam and Eve did not have a "conscience" for sin before they disobeyed God by eating from the tree of the knowledge of good and evil. Before the Fall, Adam's soul and body were completely submitted to God's Spirit. After the fall, mankind's spirit and soul became darkened by sin and were separated from God (not possessing sensitivity or conscious of God's presence). As the result, fallen man is unable to fellowship with God, and is completely governed by his fleshly and soulish desires as the Apostle Paul states in I Corintinians 2:14:

> *But the natural man receiveth not the things of the Spirit of God: for they are foolishness unto him: neither can he know them, because they are spiritually discerned.*

The Lord Jesus Christ came to earth and took man's darkened and sinful nature upon himself so that through His physical death and resurrection mankind might receive spiritual life.

> *For God so loved the world, that he gave his only begotten Son, that whosoever believeth in him should not perish, but have everlasting life.*
> (John 3:16)

Before man's spirit can have life again he must have the spirit of God within. This is what Jesus spoke to Nicodemus about in John 3:4:

> *Nicodemus saith unto him, How can a man be born when he is old? Can he enter the second time into his mother's womb, and be born?*

Of course not! It would be impossible to be born all over again. It is possible, though, to be spiritually born again and to have the life of God imparted to us. By receiving Jesus Christ as Lord and Savior, our dead spirit then receives life through the Holy Spirit and we again are able to fellowship with God.

> *Now we have received, not the spirit of the world, but the spirit which is of God; that we might know the things that are freely given to us of God.*
> (I Corinthians 2:12)

> *God is a Spirit; and they that worship him must worship him in spirit and in truth* (John 4:24).

At salvation, a person's spirit receives God's life through the Holy Spirit. Therefore, if the soulish nature is expressed through the personality (temperament), Christians have a choice to be spiritual (yielding to the Holy Spirit) or soulish (yielding to the flesh or carnal nature). If we yield to the desires of the soul and body we will be controlled by them; but if we yield to the Holy Spirit we will overcome the desires of the soul and body.

> *For they that are after the flesh do mind the things of the flesh; but they that are after the Spirit the things of the Spirit* (Romans 8:5).

If our soul life (temperament) dictates our actions, we do not live the spiritual life that God requires. Because of our fleshly weakness, God gives us the ability through the power of the Holy Spirit to be victorious over all of the desires of our old spiritual and soulish nature.

The soul is comprised of the mind, will, and emotions. The soul is then exhibited in our personality (or temperament) through our feelings, thoughts, behavior, and perceptions. Intellect, reasoning, and feelings are in the soul (or personality) and these distinquish people as unique and different individuals.

What is Typology?

Typology is the modern terminology used to identify the spirit, soul, and body. It is the philosophical attempt to explain the personality. According to modern classifications, characteristics, traits, and temperaments place individuals within a particular category which is called "type" or "typology." Typology is a psychological term describing certain characteristics which when combined comprise the basic personality. The personality is expressed through the "soul." To understand the soul is to understand the personality.

In an attempt to define the soul, many different theories evolved from the philosophy of typology. Many of these theories of personality originated from ancient civilizations and astrology.

According to the *Encyclopedia Dictionary of Psychology*, contemporary psychiatry gradually progressed within the field of medicine and separated itself from mythology and religion.[1] Unfortunately, this is not entirely true as stated by Martin and Deidre Bobgan in *Psycho Heresy*, "Psychotherapy fits more reasonably into the category of religion than into the field of science."[2] Even so, the study of the temperament was discredited many years ago because of its connection with inherited traits which contradicted behaviorism.[3]

Astrological typology originated from an ancient religious worship of the heavenlies. The beginnings of the pseudo-Hippocratic humoural typology of the temperament's remain documented in ancient historical records within the realm of mythology and the religion of astrology.

There are many other "New Age" personality systems used in describing characteristics and patterns of the personality. These systems claim to assist one in understanding disposition, in defining personal strengths and weaknesses, and provide directions on how to improve the personality. Combined with supernaturalism, these personality systems attempt to reach the inner soul and spirit to give direction and understanding to the personality. I call these New Age typology systems "Temperamysticism" and the teachers of these worldly philosophies are the spiritual "Temperamystics."

The psychologists Sigmund Freud and Carl Jung, developed personality systems which are completely opposed to Christian doctrine.

Sigmund Freud (1856-1939), the founder of modern psychoanalysis, was completely atheistic in his approach to religion, believing in the treatment of psychopathic disorders through the subconscious mind.

Carl Jung (1875-1961), a pupil of Freud, reportedly involved mysticism in his work and also possessed a mythological belief of religion. Jung's theories involved the "introvert" and "extrovert" classifications of the personality. He also revived a belief in astrology through philosophical and scientific studies on causality. Carl Jung had a deep interest in parapsychology, supernatural phenomenon, and the spiritual nature of humans.

Another form of typology is the Myers-Briggs Typology Indicator (MBTI) and is a personality system which is becoming increasingly popular especially among Christians. The MBTI, also known as the Myers-Briggs Personality Inventory, is based on the work of Carl Jung.

The Myers-Briggs Typology is a "self" assessment of basic reactions and is used in the process of understanding individual dispositions, perception, and judgment. The MBTI is predominantly used by Christians to understand their strengths and weaknesses. Very similar to the temperament theory of the personality, the MBTI attempts to merge the psychological with spiritual principles. Also, it is my opinion that the MBTI may run a close parallel to the enneagram, a typology system having its origins in Eastern mysticism.

One other personality typology recently introduced to the Christian community is the DISC formula of human behavior used in Dr. Mels Carbonell and Dr. Robert Rohm's *Personality Profile*.[4] This system is identical to the four-fold typology of the temperaments but relabeled using different terms. Based upon the book, *The Emotions of Normal People*, 1928, by William Olten Marston, the DISC formula is a system utilizing the temperament philosophy of D=choleric, I=sanguine, S=phlegmatic, and C=melancholy. This system expounds on the introvert/extrovert type of personality.

Frankly, when using this system I found it paralleled

the enneagram (to be discussed later) in its association with numbers and personality types.

Also, referred to in the children's profile was the scripture Proverbs 22:6: *Train up a child in the way he should go: and when he is old, he will not depart from it.* Does this apply to training up a child in the spiritual things of God and he will not depart from the Lord; or does this scripture apply to training up a child in the ways of the personality and he will not depart from it?

Throughout history many other typology systems developed distinguishing individuals in respect to their personality differences. Many of these systems have the uncanny ability to very closely resemble the true nature of our personality. It would be virtually impossible to compile a list of all known typologies. Typologists classify and separate individuals into almost every personality combination imaginable. Many of these personality systems overlap and duplicate one another, making them ambiguous and difficult to understand.

What is the point with all of these personality typologies? All of this discussion on typologies is enough to drive any average, level-headed Christian into a neurotic, paranoid, or manic-depressive state.

After awhile it certainly must be confusing as to which system is the right one. Of course, we don't want to forget to mention cerebral hemisphere dominance (right-brain or left-brain), past-life regression, inner healing, or perhaps even nasology (differences in the shapes and sizes of the nose). Where does it stop for the Christian? We may get so caught up in personality typologies that we forget about Jesus Christ and living the spiritual life.

New Age typologies are infiltrating and contaminating the Christian church with worldly philosophies, occult wisdoms, Eastern mysticism, pagan religions, and even witchcraft. Attempting to unite the total person, these personality theories combine an individual's physical, mental, emotional, and most importantly, spiritual nature.

There are many encouraging, uplifting, and spiritually inspiring books available to help Christians cope with everyday life. Unfortunately, in some cases, secular psychological theories are being blended with Christian doctrine to teach people how to live their lives. These books contain worldly theories based upon human traditions and values rather than the Word of God. Rather than turning to the Word of God and the transforming power of the Holy Spirit, Christians rely on these self-help, self-esteem, and self-confidence books appearing even on the shelves of Christian bookstores.

These books diametrically oppose what scripture teaches. In an attempt to assist the Christian in living a psychologically "whole" existence, Christ is placed on the outside, representing Him as a separated entity apart from mankind. As a result, the most dangerous aspect of these personality typologies is their ability to divert worship of God to adoration of the "self."

Both astrology and the temperament theory are ancient personality theories which classify and categorize individuals, forcing them into a pre-shaped mold of identification. They both represent the soul nature or the personality of the person. Both of these theories command allegiance to a predetermined set of rules of conduct. What about the intrinsic and distinctive individuality given to man from God Almighty? Each of us has a unique personality, like our one-of-a-kind fingerprint.

We are not saved to become soulical or spiritual

robots. Uniqueness is the distinctive thumbprint God imparted to the personality. No two individuals are the same physically or soulically. People come from different backgrounds, experiences, and lifestyles. People are reared in opulance and others in poverty; others are healthy and then there are the sick; the intelligent and so on. Overall, whatever the condition or situation, everyone is distinctly and uniquely different from every other person who was ever born.

For the Christian, however, it is much more important to be aware of the condition of our spiritual nature. God's Word is the divine guidance we should seek for all of our earthly living. Shouldn't the emphasis be placed on the spiritual life of a person, rather than on their flesh or outward appearance?

When Christians apply astrology signs or temperament types to their lives, they place themselves in bondage to the dictates of that particular theory. Jesus Christ came to deliver people from the bondages of sin and to *set the captive free* (Luke 4:18) because (II Corinthians 3:17) . . . *where the spirit of the Lord is, there is liberty.*

The theories of astrology and the temperaments are applied not only to the emotional or physical person but also to the spiritual nature of human beings. We cannot intersperse mystical occult wisdom with the Holy Spirit's wisdom. One comes from Satan and the other from God.

Twenty to thirty years ago, both the temperament theory and astrology had a coinciding resurgence in popularity. One should question why the temperament theory (based on occult precepts) is so popular among Christians? Is the temperament theory a planned deception by Satan to introduce ancient worldly philosophies into the lives of Christians? Is it possible this simultaneous occurrence is mere coincidence, or could this be a significant event dealing with end-time prophecy?

10

The Enneagram, Astrology, and the Temperaments

Where is the wise? where is the scribe? where is the disputer of this world? hath not God made foolish the wisdom of this world?
I Corinthians 1:20

The New Age of understanding "the self" has emerged. People want to know about themselves and others. It is the mystical aspect of the soul and body which the New Agers attempt to unite with the spiritual part of a person. The New Agers believe one can unite the spirit by merging the soul and body together. Supposedly, through meditation, yoga, transpersonal identities (such as spiritual guides), universalistic thought, mind-over-matter and other mystical philosophies, one will be united with the cosmos and nature.

TEMPERAMYSTICISM

Mystic hopefuls perceive man as a god, therefore man possesses all control over his destiny and his spirit-life independent from responsibility between the relationship of God to mankind. Rather than becoming interdependent upon God through the power of the Holy Spirit, one is taught to subconsciously search within their inner being seeking unity between themselves and the god of self. By being in touch with one's inner being, one is placed in harmony with the universe. The one, true God is not considered as part of the process. A higher consciousness is in actuality a self-consciousness whereby one exalts himself to the position of God.

Many of the typologies of today are duplicates of the Graeco-Roman myths, Eastern mysticism, and ancient occult wisdoms. By placing one's spirit at the core and center of the "self," the modern typologies focus upon energies that are manifested within the soul. The soul, being in a position to be influenced by Satanic powers, will naturally yield to whatever satisfies the emotional or physical need at a particular moment. For example, if someone is emotionally distraught and they meditate, concentrating on a focal point and yielding their soul to unknown entities, they open themselves to demonic suggestion or possession. They are freeing their soul to accept any thought or feeling which comes to them during meditation. The soul is, therefore, susceptible, and has a greater sensitivity, to thoughts that may not originate from the person but from an outside source.

In this way Satan is able to control the soul life of an unbeliever, or even a believer. A person without Christ does not possess a renewed spirit and is, therefore, unable to hear the Holy Spirit's guidance. The Holy Spirit does not dwell within that person to guide them intuitively. Fortunately, a believer who is listening to the Holy Spirit's promptings will not yield to outside influences or to soulish thoughts. Listening to the Holy Spirit within our conscience tells us whether or not what we hear is, or is not, the truth according to the Word of God. By listening and obeying the Holy Spirit's promptings according to the Word of God enables a Christian to live a spiritual life.

New Age Typology of The Enneagram

The enneagram represents one of the New Age typologies gaining recognition and acceptance in many denominations of Christianity. The ancient enneagram philosophy merges with Christianity by uniting Biblical truths with Greek philosophy, astrology, numerology, and modern psychology.

Limited historical information regarding the enneagram's origins most likely contributes to a certain mystique surrounding its philosophical doctrines. The enneagram gives the appearance of spirituality, shrouded in the secrecy of Eastern mysticism and ancient occult wisdoms. This mystical study of the personality for the most part is verbally passed from teacher to student.

No one really knows were the enneagram came from, but it is believed to have originated around the 14th or 15th Century by mystics called the Sufis and the Jesuits. Personally, from research, this author believes that much of the enneagram's modern philosophy came from Pythagoras.

Pythagoras' system was a combination of philosophy, religion, and science. He assigned numbers to the ancient Greek gods. Therefore, the highest divinity would be associated with the number "One" while lesser gods are associated with higher consecutive numbers. Therefore, "One" was associated with the supreme divinity. The basic concept of the enneagram is the association of numbers with the higher and lower personality.

The magnetic spiritual teacher, George I. Gurdjieff (approximately 1877-1949), first coined the name enneagram. Oscar Ichazo reportedly is the founder of Arica Institute and the most recent leader of this group acquiring his knowledge from the same school that Gurdjieff attended.

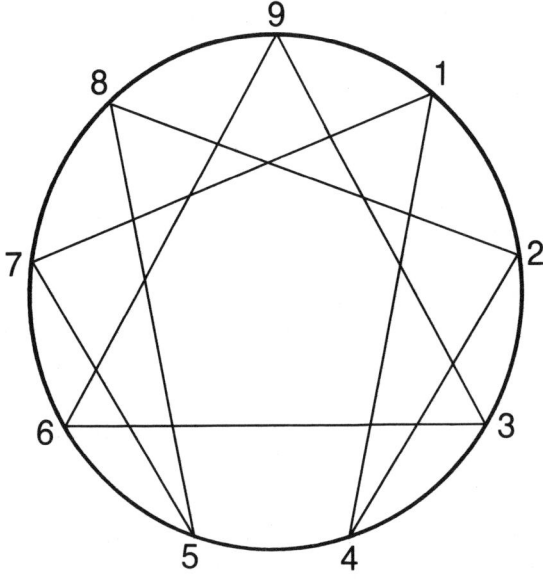

The enneagram is a complex geometric design of triads, angles and numbers combined with astrological symbols. The Greek word "ennea" means nine, and its appearance is that of a diagram, which is why it is called "enneagram." The nine intersecting lines which interrelate represent nine personality types. When combined, individuals will be a mixture of two of these types.

THE ENNEAGRAM, ASTROLOGY, AND THE TEMPERAMENTS

The same duplicity found in astrology and the temperaments is a typical aspect of most of the New Age typologies combining one or more traits blended together to provide basic personality descriptions.

The enneagram's philosophy concerns the mind, perception, and the formulation of judgments. The goal is to reach several states of consciousness and to discern the true self from the false self. As with the temperaments, the enneagram promotes understanding our personality flaws, strengths/weaknesses through the transformation of negative characteristics into positive ones.

The enneagram claims to represent the nine facets of God's image. Within the nine facets both positive and negative personality characteristics are listed (the nine positive facets are a duplication of the nine Fruit of the Holy Spirit). Supposedly, those who participate in God's nature have acquired portions of the nine manifestations of God. The ultimate goal is to express one of these facets through their own personality.

The enneagram philosophy claims that our natural weaknesses limit the expression of God's true qualities through our personality. Understanding the enneagram professes to place one in touch with their genuine self (inner man). At the point of surrender to one's self the enneagram assists in manifesting God's image in realizing an individual's full potential and thereby places one in harmony with the cosmos (outer man).

The enneagram is a mystical attempt at understanding oneself. It is a process whereby one seeks deeper and deeper self-analysis and self-transformation to strive towards a harmonious relationship with ones' self never obtaining total perfection or wholeness with nature. The enneagram's philosophy compares to a futile search for righteousness; continually struggling in desperation to reach the top of a spiritual mountain but never quite grasping the truth.

Texe Marrs in *Mystery Mark of the New Age* explains how the enneagram is so popular among Catholic charismatics.

> "A Catholic priest, Reverend Jim Cook, is giving special seminars. He calls the enneagram 'a system of spiritual self-discovery.' Cook teaches that the enneagram identifies nine basic personality types, the compulsions of each, their causes and how to spiritually overcome these compulsions. Somehow this New Age cleric even ties in the personality traits of Jesus."[1]

The New Age Temperamystics, endeavoring to legitimize their theories, associate the personality and temperament traits with Jesus . Presumably, by relating personality theories with the Name and Divine traits of Jesus gives credibility which, therefore, encourages Christians to accept these doctrines as being scripturally correct.

The dangers of the enneagram are obvious. We cannot reach God through inner consciousness and self-awareness. God has made it clear that the only way to reach the Father is through His Son, Jesus Christ, as stated in John 1:12-13 (NIV); *. . . all who received him, to those who believed in his name, he gave the right to become children of God—children born not of natural descent, nor of human decision or a husband's will, but born of God.* Also John 3:3 (NIV); *. . . Jesus declared, "I tell you the truth, unless a man is born again, he cannot see the kingdom of God."*

Only when we have Jesus Christ do we have the Father and the Holy Spirit. When we have the Fruit of the Spirit we have the gifts of the Spirit. God does not want us to be self-conscious but God-conscious dying to our natural self and living our Christian life separated unto God.

The enneagram and the temperaments portray only two New Age typologies gaining popularity within the last few years. Out of all personality systems, astrology is the oldest form of personality typology.

All of the New Age typologies—the enneagram, astrology, and the temperaments—have origins deeply imbedded in the occult. Each one of these theories attempt to enable one to reach a "higher" or "holier" existence by understanding and applying its concepts. The New Age temperamystics are teaching people how to better understand one's self. As Christians we should seek to know and become more like Christ. This is God-consciousness, not self-consciousness. **The temperaments belong to astrology and not Christianity.**

Where Did Astrology Originate?

The ancient religion of astrology was predicated upon the belief in the divinity of the planetary heavens. In ancient history, men established the worship of the "hosts of heaven," the sky, the four elements (earth, air, fire, and water), time, and all of nature. The Old Testament clearly communicated in warnings against the worship of the heavens attesting to the fact that the ancient civilizations believed in astrology.

> . . . *Therefore watch yourselves very carefully, so that you do not become corrupt and make for yourselves an idol . . . And when you look up to the sky and see the sun, the moon and the stars—all the heavenly array—do not be enticed into bowing down to them and worshiping things the Lord your God has apportioned to all the nations under heaven* (Deuteronomy 4:15-19).

TEMPERAMYSTICISM

Astrology originated and flourished in the ancient city of Babylon, located between the Euphrates and Tigris rivers in Mesopotamia over 4,000 years ago. The powerful empire, Babylon where Satan ruled and every imaginable wickedness existed. Demonic activity engulfed the religion of the ancient Babylonians where demonic powers were manifested through witchcraft, the worship of the heavens and nature, divination, black magic, and demon worship. The evil of Babylon is clearly illustrated in the Book of Revelation, *. . . is become the habitation of devils, and the hold of every foul spirit, and a cage of every unclean and hateful bird* (Revelations 18:2).

Although Babylon was at one time the greatest and most magnificent city in the world, it was completely destroyed by approximately 165 A.D.; only the smoldering ruins of the Babylonian empire remained visible as a remnant of its existence. God's anger burned against Babylon, Chaldea, and Assyria because of idolatry and the worship of the heavens.

> *. . . her foundations are fallen, her walls are thrown down: for it is the vengeance of the Lord: take vengeance upon her; as she hath done, do unto her* (Jeremiah 50:15).
>
> *A sword is upon the Chaldeans, saith the Lord, and upon the inhabitants of Babylon, and upon her princes, and upon her wise men* (Jeremiah 50:35).

Judgment was against the land and people who practiced the worship of the heavenly hosts (astrology). The Bible speaks many times of God being the *Lord of hosts*. The hosts represented the sun, moon, planets and stars. *. . . for this is the work of the Lord God of hosts in the land of the Chaldeans* (Jeremiah 50:25).

God is a jealous God and warned that we should have no other Gods before him.

THE ENNEAGRAM, ASTROLOGY, AND THE TEMPERAMENTS

> *Thou shalt not make thee any graven image, or any likeness of any thing that is in heaven above, or that is in the earth beneath, or that is in the waters beneath the earth. Thou shalt not bow down thyself unto them, nor serve them: for I the Lord thy God am a jealous God* . . . (Deuteronomy 5:8,9).

Astrology founded idolatry, the worship of other gods. The children of Israel were told over and over again by the Lord God Jehovah to separate themselves from the heathen practice of worshipping the heavenly hosts and the elements of earth, fire, air, and water.

Prophets and priests of the heathen nations attempted to turn the children of Israel away from the ways of the Lord.

> *. . . you must not listen to the words of that prophet or dreamer. The Lord your God is testing you to find out whether you love him with all your heart and with all your soul. It is the Lord your God you must follow, and him you must revere* . . . (Deuteronomy 13:3-4 NIV).

God knew of the idolatrous people who dwelled in the land promised to the Israelites. . . . *the Hittites, Girgashites, Amorites, Canaanites, Perizzsites, Hivites and Jebusites* (Deuteronomy 7:1), were delivered by God into the hands of Israel. The evil of these nations threatened to corrupt God's people, so they must be destroyed before the Israelites could inhabit the land.

> *The Lord your God will cut off before you the nations you are about to invade and dispossess. But when you have driven them out and settle in their land, and after they have been destroyed before you, be careful not to be ensnared by inquiring about their gods, saying, 'How do these nations serve their gods? We will do the same.' You must not worship the Lord your God in their way, because in worshiping their gods, they do all kinds*

> *of detestable things the Lord hates. They even burn their sons and daughters in the fire as sacrifices to their gods* (Deuteronomy 12:29-31).

The idolatrous nations which the children of Israel dispossessed practiced astrology, sorcery, and divination.

> *... Let no one be found among you who sacrifices his son or daughter in the fire, who practices divination or sorcery, interprets omens, engages in witchcraft, or casts spells, or who is a medium or spiritist or who consults the dead ...* (Deuteronomy 10:10-13).

Any prophet who spoke in the Lord's name falsely, proclaiming something which did not take place, was put to death. This was a false prophet who spoke lies to lead the people into worshipping other gods.

Throughout the Old Testament God performed many miracles in the sight of the Israelites. He alone was God over all of nature, creation, and Lord over the elements of earth, fire, air, and water. He separated the mighty waters of the Red Sea (water); He went before the children of Israel in "fire" by night and a cloud (air) by day; God gave them the land before them to possess (earth)—(Deuteronomy 1, and Psalm 114 and 115). In all ways God proved rulership of the heavens and earth.

> *Has any god ever tried to take for himself one nation out of another nation, by testing, by miraculous signs and wonders, by war, by a mighty hand and an outstretched arm, or by great and awesome deeds, like all the things the Lord your God did for you in Egypt before your very eyes? You were shown these things so that you might know that the Lord is God; besides him there is no other. From heaven he made you hear his voice to discipline you ...* (Deuteronomy 4:34-39 NIV).

The Ancient Astrologers

The ancient civilizations' understanding of God and nature was comprised of their belief in the divinity of the heavenly bodies. One can understand and appreciate the awe of the ancients when gazing heavenward on a star-filled night. This heavenly showcase lent to the ardent devotion evoked in the ancient civilizations resulting in their worship of the heavens.

This ancient astral religion of astrology did not recognize the Creator, the true and living God (Jehovah), as the creator of His universe. Thus, astrology became the worship of God's creation rather than God the Creator. The truth of God was changed into a lie because the ancients . . . *worshipped and served the creature more than the Creator, who is blessed forever* (Romans 1:25). The prophet Isaiah expressed this in clear detail: *Lift up your eyes and look to the heavens: Who created all these? He who brings the starry host one by one, and calls them each by name* (Isaiah 40:26).

The Bible states the existence of God is proven in all of nature because the order of life and all systems are proof of His existence. *For the invisible things of him from the creation of the world are clearly seen, being understood by the things that are made, even his eternal power and Godhead; so that they are without excuse* (Romans 1:20).

Astrology originated as an idolatrous form of worship permeating ancient religions and superstitions. This ancient mystic belief elevated Time to a place of divinity. As Franz Cumont expressed in *Astrology and Religion Among the Greeks and Romans,* "It was the heavenly bodies that by their regular movements taught man to divide into successive sections the unbroken chain of moments."[2] The worship of the planets and heavens resulted in "Fate" and "Destiny" becoming the lord over their lives, abolishing free-will.

Astrology is mystical Babylon. Compulsive and addicting, it draws and entices its victims into a spider's web oblivious to the trap. This ancient religion is like an evil seductress who uses witchcraft to cast her spell. The belief in astrology renders mankind helpless to "Fate" and a predetermined "Destiny." Astrology places the lofty dome above as the master puppeteer and humans on earth below as mere puppets who are manipulated and controlled by occurrences in the changing appearance of the heavens. People become robots who obey every command and passively yield to the inevitable results of their astrology chart.

Saint Augustine (354 A.D.) wrote three books on astrology, pagan gods, and religion *(The Confessions, The City of God,* and *On Christian Doctrine).*

At first Augustine believed and practiced astrology, but later became a staunch opponent and disbeliever. He refuted this idolatrous religion in his fifth book of the *City of God,* stating that he defended man's freedom of will. God held each person accountable for their choice to do good or evil.

In *On Superstition,* Saint Augustine writes on astrologers, "they attempt thence to predict our actions, or the consequences of our actions, grievously err, and sell inexperienced men into a miserable bondage."[3]

Astrology is linked throughout history with astronomy, meteorology, medicine, physics, and mathematics. This astrological conception of life and the world permeated the whole of ancient societies. Throughout ancient history thoughts, beliefs, practices and branches of science were directly connected to this astral conception of the universe which spread throughout Egypt, the Orient, the Aztecs, Arabia, China,

India and became a significant belief in the Middle Ages, the Renaissance and eventually throughout the world.

Astrology and divination were the supernatural tools used in guiding and dictating the actions and future happenings of everyday ancient life. Man's fate remained fixed according to the planetary positions within the constellation.

Magic and Astrology

Magic, superstition, and astrology infused with all ancient pagan religious belief. Astrology (horoscopia) or the observation of nativities is an integral part of magic. The word magic means sorcery and the art of producing supernatural results through occult arts and superstitions. Lynn Thorndike quotes in his writings on magic as:

> "... false in its professions, mistress of all iniquity and malice, deceiving concerning the truth and truly doing harm; it seduces souls from divine religion, promotes the worship of demons, engenders corruption of morals, and impels the minds of its followers to every crime and abomination."[4]

Babylon and Assyria, as stated earlier, gained recognition as the "beginnings of astrology." Cumont stated, "Babylon was the mother of astronomy, star-worship, and astrology, that thence these sciences and these beliefs spread over the world . . . ."[5]

> *And I heard another voice from heaven, saying, Come out of her, my people, that ye be not partakers of her sins, and that ye receive not of her plagues. For her sins have reached into heaven, and God hath remembered her iniquities.*
> (Revelations 18:4-5).

Astrology Today

Throughout history astrology continues to hold a curious interest for many people. Today the revival of this ancient Babylonian religion is found in many different forms of the occult.

Astrology slowly gained popularity during the 1960's and became the national "craze." Many people called this time period the dawning of the "Age of Aquarius" (approximately 2000 A.D. to 4000 A.D.). During the 1960's and 1970's, the hope for a world of peace, love, and harmony existed in the hearts of all people. The search for tranquility unfortunately led many to Satan whose great disguise became the drug culture, free-living, and the cause of bondage and entrapment. In actuality, this was the dawning of the New Age Movement.

The popularity of astrology throughout the nation today is obvious when we open our daily newspapers and look under the heading "Daily Horoscope." The daily horoscope, however, is an inadequate representation of the serious professional astrologer who spends considerable time and detail studying the stars and focusing on an individual's life and destiny. Many astrology enthusiasts are unable to make decisions unless first consulting their favorite astrologers for daily, monthly, or yearly prognostications for the future.

According to a 1975 Gallup Poll, 32 million Americans believe the stars influence people's lives.[6] This same poll indicated that over 70 per cent of all Americans know their astrology sign (sun sign). Astrology touches many lives whether in poverty or power. It is tempting to want to know what tomorrow brings. We as Christians must rest in the thought that God holds our tomorrows and we have mercy for today. Christians must live one day at a time trusting God for the future.

Astrology and the Temperaments

Each sign of the zodiac has a ruling god overseeing the destiny of a person's life. As a part of astrology, the temperament theory in reality is a branch of the occult. Each sign in astrology corresponds to one of the four elements or gods of Empedocles. Each of the god-elements rules over a temperament type.

Most temperament enthusiasts maintain the reliability of the temperament concept, its accuracy in explaining the differences among individuals. The temperaments being a part of astrology gives evidence that many things in the occult world do work. They have the appearance of truth. Mostly astrology works because those involved want it to.

The temperament theory is interwoven and combined with astrology in describing the personality characteristics and traits of different individuals.

Many Christians spend more time and effort to learn about their temperament and develop the fleshly nature than studying the Word of God to strengthen their spiritual nature. The reason for this is because the occult heritage of the temperaments is intimately associated with divination through astrology.

Ask any temperament enthusiast to give up the temperaments. Not only will there be anger and defensiveness, but a great deal of defiance. The temperaments are as witchcraft because they are so intimately tied to astrology: enticing, demonic, and very difficult to relinquish. The compulsion to continue involvement with this theory will always be a temptation unless it is totally renounced. This explains the addictive, compulsive, and demonic control the temperament theory has over the lives of Christians who submit to its doctrines. No matter how Christians testify to how the temperaments have helped them and revealed to them differences in the personality it does not change the fact that the temperaments are tied to the occult.

Astrology Signs

Fire signs: Aries, Leo, and Sagittarius
Air signs: Gemini, Libra, and Aquarius
Earth signs: Taurus, Virgo, and Capricorn
Water signs: Cancer, Scorpio, and Pisces

Astrology Signs & The Temperaments

Fire signs: Aries, Leo, and Sagittarius = **Choleric**
Air signs: Gemini, Libra, and Aquarius = **Sanguine**
Earth signs: Taurus, Virgo, and Capricorn = **Phlegmatic**
Water signs: Cancer, Scorpio, and Pisces = **Melancholy**

11
Conclusion

> *And if a kingdom be divided against itself, that kingdom cannot stand. And if a house be divided against itself, that house cannot stand. And if Satan rise up against himself, and be divided, he cannot stand, but hath an end.*
>
> Mark 3:24-26

Astrology is an occult religion which incorporated the elemental deities worshipped in ancient and medieval civilizations. The elemental deities are the philosophical roots of the temperament theory. The elemental deities of earth, fire, air, and water were thought to be the substances composing all of man, nature, and the entire universe. As the result of this philosophical belief, to the pagan, astrology maintained occult supremacy regulating the lives of mankind, moving through the elements to determine the nature of the temperament and bodily constitution, and lastly, considered to be the unerring power to control mankind's Destiny.

It is contradictory to accept the temperament theory of the personality and yet deny its astrological roots. This apparent inconsistency is representative of the kingdom of the temperaments being divided against itself, and although Christians denounce astrology and the occult, they accept the doctrine of the temperaments upon which astrology originated.

For the most part, ancient and medieval medicine combined experimental research and science mixed with astrology, mythology, superstition, magic, and religion. In the Twentieth Century, astrology, the elemental deities, and the temperament theory are not recognized as a viable part of modern chemistry or medical science.

Regardless of the evidence, even from a non-Christian perspective indicating astrology is a false science, the astrologer's still devotedly adhere to the concept of the four elements. The summation of this is clearly evident in Roger Culver and Philip Ianna's *Astrology True or False:*

> "... despite the fact that as any elementary chemistry student can attest, each of these basic elements is itself made up of two or more of the 104 currently recognized chemical elements. Each element of course can also exist in one of three basic phases gas, liquid and solid, depending on its surrounding temperature and pressure. Thus Aristotle's four element model holds little more than historical interest for the modern chemist."[1]

The *Encyclopedia of Psychology* mentions that while the humoural doctrine could no longer be taken seriously, the work of our philosophical ancestors could possibly have inspired contemporary researchers to look for biochemical sources of variations in human behavior.[2]

CONCLUSION

Not only does modern philosophy, for the most part, reject the idea of the temperaments, but Bible scholars, theologians, and even the average Bible student would be hard pressed to find even a remote scriptural truth in favor of the temperaments. The temperaments have no scriptural foundation that make this theory relevant to Christianity.

Here is where Satan enters. He desires to draw Christians away from the truth and also to entice Christians into concentrating on their carnal natures rather than obtaining a closer relationship with God. Worldly Christians are ineffective spiritually. Satan through the temperament theory will create a bunch of milk-toast, whimpy Christians who can be manipulated and controlled through their flesh nature.

If the ancient temperament philosophy has been scorned by modern philosophers, then the only groups using this theory are the Christians. In essence, the world renounced its own temperament philosophy and Christianity eagerly accepts what the worldly conceived and disgarded.

Christians who study and practice the temperaments are using a theory abandoned by modern medicine for over 400 years. The ancient religions have been replaced by secular humanism and its modern-day counterpart the "New Age" movement. The New Age philosophers attach their own theories to philosophy which are more current with humanistic trends.

If the roots of the temperament theory are deeply imbedded in the worship of the ancient Graeco-Roman elemental dieties of earth, air, fire, and water, and we use the temperament theory as part of our Christian learning, then why not include astrology? They both have the same heritage. How does a Christian apply ancient anti-Christian philosophical theories in living a Christian life, when those same theories teach doctrine which is diametrically opposed to the Word of God?

The temperaments for the Christian is a contamination of worldliness, not the obvious—such as openly living in sin—but the captivating worldliness of "carnality." The temperament concept is easy to justify because it appeals to the senses. It's the worldliness of secular humanism: If it *works,* it must be good!

Jesus Christ's kingdom is not of this world. Christians are to be in the world but not of it. Revival breaks forth only when Christians are the most unworldly. Unworldliness creates an influence affecting the unsaved and firing up the passive Christian. This influence is the setting-aside, crucifying, of the fleshly nature and allowing the Holy Spirit to love through the Christian to an unsaved world. Jesus Christ began the love principle during His ministry on this earth which was to continue through His body, the Church, after He ascended into heaven.

It would virtually be impossible to find scriptures to support the temperament theory, but there are scriptural references which speak against idolatry and the worship of the elements.

The heavenly planets were thought to contain the four elements of the world, "stichia tou kosmou," the heavens, and mankind existing within the universe. Paul speaks of the elemental deities in Galatians 4:3 and Galatians 4:8-10. These were the fundamental principles of which Paul speaks.

Paul mentions it is time for Christians to grow up into maturity, to leave the former ways of living because in Christ, we are no longer under bondage but free. Paul is writing about the elemental spirits which belong to the world's philosophy.

CONCLUSION

> *Even so we, when we were children, were in bondage under the **elements** of the world:* (Galatians 4:3).
>
> *Howbeit then, when ye knew not God, ye did service unto them which by nature are no gods. But now, after that ye have known God, or rather are known of God, how turn ye again to the weak and beggarly **elements**, whereunto ye desire again to be in bondage? Ye observe days, and months, and times, and years* (Galatians 4:8-10).

The last verse, *Ye observe days, and months, and times, and years,* is the ancient Graeco-Roman religious worship of the cosmic elemental deities and the observation of Time as a deified power. These references make implication to the astrological powers of the heavens which determine the calendar and rule over festivals and ritual worship (Colossians 2:16). In following the rules and regulations of the stars, one is placing himself in bondage to the dictates of astrology and philosophy (Colossians 2:8, 20-23, 3:2-3).

What will the astrologers say on the day of the Lord? At His coming the planets and stars in heaven will vanish, the sun will be darkened and the moon will no longer shed its light. Astrologers, fortune tellers, and mediums attempt to predict the future but only the Lord God in heaven holds the future.

In II Peter 3:10, Peter writes of the elements in the universe and at the end of time how they will be destroyed.

> *But the day of the Lord will come as a thief in the night; in the which the heavens shall pass away with a great noise, and the **elements** shall melt with fervent heat, the earth also and the works that are therein shall be burned up.*

Nothing will stand on that day. The mighty hand of the Lord will rule, and evidence of his omnipotent power and might will be displayed in the destruction of the idolatrous worship of the heavens, the elements including the earth and all that dwells within it.

> *Looking for and hasting unto the coming of the day of God, wherein the heavens being on fire shall be dissolved, and the **elements** shall melt with fervent heat?* (II Peter 3:12).

In Revelation 16, the vials of wrath were poured out upon nature, mankind, and all of the elements. The first vial was poured out upon the *earth,* the second and third vial were poured out upon the *waters,* the fourth vial was poured out upon the sun, *fire,* and the seventh vial was poured out upon the *air.* The vials of wrath manifested the power God has over the elements, since he created them, yet men have made them gods, instead of serving the God who created them.

After the vials of wrath are poured out follows the "judgment of the great whore" which is Babylon, "the mother of harlots and abominations of the earth." This is the Great Babylon where judgment has fallen; Satan's throne where all evil flourished and abounded. Babylon where mankind surrendered to every desire of the flesh; corrupted hearts, seared consciousness, and where only the remnants of human kindness surrendered to animal lusts. Witchcraft, divination, and idolatry, the fruits of Babylon's wickedness contaminate the whole world from its beginnings.

Is this the heritage Christians want? Then, why the temperaments?

World Wisdoms and Christianity

The temperaments, like astrology, are very intriguing and undoubtedly stimulate the curiosity of any individual wanting to understand the deeper meanings

CONCLUSION

of the "self." As Christians, the Bible is very clear in stating that we must constantly put the "self" under submission to the Holy Spirit. The temperament concept places the self first by concentrating on how to better oneself rather than concentrating on how to be spiritually mature.

This self-understanding only places Christians in bondage and imprisons the true person, which is the spirit-man, from taking preeminence in one's life. As Galatians 3:3 expresses, *Are ye so foolish? Having begun in the Spirit are ye now made perfect by the flesh?*

The Bible speaks often about the flesh but always in the context of *keeping it under* or *crucifying* or *clothing with righteousness.* The Bible tells us to diminish the self-life and to seek the spiritual life as in Ephesians 4:22-24,

> *You were taught, with regard to your former way of life, to put off your old self, which is being corrupted by its deceitful desires; to be made new in the attitude of your minds; and to put on the new self, created to be like God in true righteousness and holiness.*

What difference does it make whether we are a sanguine or phlegmatic or whatever? If we are in Christ walking in the Spirit with the Fruit of the Spirit in evidence, ideally we will walk in Love with others, especially Christians, because we will be the same in the divine nature of Christ.

When the Holy Spirit indwells a believer there is a similarity. It doesn't matter what temperament a person is because there is a Christlikeness that unites all of us into one Holy Spirit temperament. This is not to say we are not to be an individual, but we must not place so much emphasis on our carnal nature. It doesn't matter how much we try to understand our carnal nature, it's still sinful. It is the Spirit of God which transforms us. This transformation is on the inside and not in our attempts to make the flesh holy. It can't be done.

Love unites and there is a commonality in Love. True Love is selfless. Christ is the example of that love and he is the example that all Christians should be reaching to attain. Where is love in the temperaments? Where is peace or joy in the temperaments? There isn't any love or peace or joy in our temperaments because the Fruit of the Spirit is not a part of our fleshly nature but is only imparted by God through the Holy Spirit to our spiritual nature . . . *for love comes from God* . . . (I John 4:7-8, 20).

Continually concentrating on fleshly incompatibilities blinds Christians to the real reason for disagreements or problems. We have problems in our flesh because we are not walking in our Christlikeness state. When we hate or when we love it doesn't come directly from our personalities, these emotions are a result of our spiritual condition. If we have the Spirit of God we have the nature of God imparted to us. When we have the nature of God in our spirits we are transformed into his temperament. The warfare is between our fleshly nature which is in direct opposition to the Holy Spirit of God. His nature is the Fruit of the Spirit and when we choose to walk in His nature our human spirit is in submission to God. If we choose to walk in our human nature we will walk according to the carnal nature which is sinful.

Satan's greatest weapon is to attack mankind's relationship to God. The enemy's foremost desire is to disfigure the image of God. Anything he can do to totally destroy relationships between husband and wife, parents and children, Christians with each other and

CONCLUSION

with God, will satisfy Satan's hunger for separation. Separation and alienation through strife brings enmity and is usually brought about because of "selfishness." The "I" principle. I want my way, I will do this . . . .

Our relationship to God is first based upon the selfless act of Jesus Christ in loving mankind all the way to the cross. If Jesus is first in our hearts, desiring to please him, the self is pushed out of the way.

In heaven there will be many different people but do you think that we will have temperaments there? Of course not! Those who are in heaven will have bodies, but our personality will be representative of the Fruit of the Spirit . . . *ourselves also, which have the firstfruits of the Spirit, even we ourselves groan within ourselves, waiting for the adoption, to wit, the redemption of our body* (Romans 8:23). In this respect we will be like Jesus Christ *But every man in his own order: Christ the firstfruits; afterward they that are Christ's at his coming* (I Corinthians 15:23). We are learning to live the spiritual life in heaven while we are here on earth *seek ye first the kingdom of God . . .* (Matthew 6:33). In heaven there will be a oneness among us because there is only one God and He has imparted His nature to us which will unite us together with Him.

When a person is born again, the personality is modified as that person matures, becoming more like Christ—when they become more Christlike. *For we know that our old self was crucified with him so that the body of sin might be rendered powerless, that we should no longer be slaves to sin . . .* (Romans 6:6 NIV). As Christians we are *Not to conform any longer to the pattern of this world, but be transformed by the renewing of your mind* (Romans 12:2 NIV).

Our concern should not be where we fit into the four temperaments but that our temperament should be that of the Fruit of the Holy Spirit. *But the Fruit of the Spirit is love, joy, peace, patience, kindness, goodness, faithfulness, gentleness and self-control* (Galatians 5:22 NIV).

Do you suppose there is an overriding master or divine temperament that Jesus gave us? In temperament classes I have heard questions asked about Jesus and his temperament type. Others have stated that Jesus was a combination of all four of the temperaments. Nonsense! Do you see what is happening here? The temperament enthusiasts are attempting to incorporate Jesus' nature into the temperaments. His nature was not fleshly, but divine! By studying the temperaments instead of the Bible, Christians will remain carnal because they are placing emphasis on obtaining divine knowledge through fleshly principles. However, we mature spiritually not by fleshly theories but through prayer, obedience to the Holy Spirit and by knowing the Word of God. If we want a temperament more like Jesus then we need to do what the Bible says, *Your attitude should be the same as that of Christ Jesus* (Philippians 2:5 NIV).

If Satan convinces people to look at their temperaments and to concentrate on what temperament type they are, he has succeeded in distracting or pulling that person farther away from the Truth. Satan desires to cause confusion to the work of the Holy Spirit. He has deceived many into thinking that this teaching is a worthwhile endeavor, when in reality it is detracting and de-emphasizing the importance of Christians becoming like Christ. This theory emphasizes the flesh person when we are to learn more about the person of Jesus Christ.

When a person steps into a room full of Christians who are completely dedicated to the Lord and full of the Holy Spirit, serving Him in obedience, and walking in the Fruit of the Spirit, he can't help but notice the unity among them. There is peace and unity where there is Love. This kind of love can only come from God through the power of the Holy Spirit. Petty differences and personalities aren't as important. In China, Brazil, America, or anywhere else, people who worship God in Spirit and in truth have one thing in common, the preeminence of the Holy Spirit. The flesh has been downplayed. They are less outwardly and more inwardly. The flesh has been cast down and the most important thing is that our concentration and worship is on God and not on ourselves.

The four temperaments nurture the flesh, by continually studying and analyzing this philosophy it keeps a Christian in the flesh rather than in the Spirit. The temperaments bring out our carnal nature which is supposed to be crucified rather than our spiritual nature which is supposed to be resurrected.

The temperament theory reflects the first Adam's temperament which was of the flesh. The Fruit of the Spirit or Christlikeness reflects the master or divine temperament which is the second Adam's—that of Christ—and that is the spiritual temperament. The first, of Adam, is of the flesh and temporal and the second, of Christ, is spiritual and eternal. The divine and master temperament of Christ is for Christians to have the character and temperament of Christ.

Satan wants to stop the Christian and what better way of doing it than with distractions. We must walk in the Spirit before our spiritual enemy Satan can be overcome; *submit yourselves therefore to God. Resist the devil, and he will flee from you* (James 4:7).

Spiritual growth is what Satan wants to hinder. Christians cannot presume they are spiritual because

TEMPERAMYSTICISM

they love God. Satan controls people through their soul life and he can only manipulate a Christian through the soul. A soulish-minded Christian has no power to overcome the enemy and no victory in their spiritual life. A powerless Christian is useless in spiritual warfare.

The New Age movement is slowly attempting to infiltrate your church, your family, and your relationship with God. Satan wants a worldly church. Seducing spirits are deceiving God's people by enticing them away from God's truth (I Timothy 4:1). Christians must know the Word of God to discern the "true'" from the "false." For this reason, we must identify from a Biblical viewpoint the validity of the temperaments comparing this theory and its origination with scriptures.

The Bible teaches Christians to follow God's principles and not the vivid, captivating personalities of temperament teachers. Are we as Christians so bored with the Word of God that we need to add a little excitement to the Bible? Have we gone so far that we are no longer interested in hearing the truths of the Bible taught in our churches?

This is so important because that is how Satan slowly deceives and corrupts. He doesn't walk in loudly and announce, "I'm here to lead you astray." He doesn't tell you he wants you carnally minded because his true deceptive nature would be revealed and then you would know what he is trying to accomplish. Satan quietly, secretly sneaks in the door with new ideas, traditions, and new ways of thinking.

The four temperament theory was conceived and taught by ungodly men. Men who believed in many gods and deities. If this is so, how can we learn spiritual truths from unsaved men?

When we accept Christ and become born again we

CONCLUSION

are baptized in water. The water baptism is symbolic of the burial of the dead body and resurrection of Jesus Christ. *We are buried with him by baptism into death: that like as Christ was raised up from the dead* (Romans 6:4). When beleivers are baptized in water it parallels what happened to Jesus Christ in his death for our sins, burial, and then his resurrection and victory over sin. The power of sin was broken and *Knowing this, that our old man is crucified with him, that the body of sin might be destroyed, that henceforth we should not serve sin* (Romans 6:6).

When churches place so much emphasis on the four temperaments, they are still living in a pre-born again experience. It's as if they are still concerned about the old nature. They have lost sight of the importance in following after the example of Christ. The following is as He died to Himself on the cross, He was buried which is symbolic of death over Himself, and His resurrection is symbolic of the way we should follow after Him. The emphasis should not be on our old nature, but on the divine nature Jesus has provided for us. Christlikeness is the divine spiritual temperament not the four temperaments. Christlikeness is the new master temperament for Christians to display.

It's been said that Moses has one type of temperament or Paul another, but the emphasis of the Bible is not on their personalities, but on their spiritual nature and relationship to God.

What we should emphasize is the Christlikeness of Paul, and not whether he was a choleric personality. We need to look at the process where Paul was converted to being a martyr in Rome, and that over a period of time if we were to look at his life; yes, he had a certain individuality but most importantly, he said that he must die daily which means he must be rid of his old nature or temperament. The fleshly person of Paul had to die so that Christ could be seen through Paul's life.

Jesus' teaching and the world's standards totally conflict. Jesus said, *Ye shall know them by their fruits* (Matthew 7:16). If we are walking in the Spirit, people will see mercy, love, compassion, unselfishness and all of the characteristics of God. Peter said we are to be "imitators of God." God's Spirit is not represented as one of the four temperaments. When people have the divine spiritual temperament of Christ it won't be necessary to ask, "What is your temperament?" Because what this question really means is, "What is you carnal walk?"

Satan's Plan to Deceive

Inconceivable as it might seem, the occult beliefs of astrology, witchcraft, and other New Age sciences, are attempting to infiltrate and influence Christian doctrine. We need to be armed with knowledge and discernment to be able to uncover Satan's schemes. Most of all, Christians need to have the power of God through the Holy Spirit operating in their lives so that we can expose Satan and his continuous attempts to deceive.

Satan has a plan for controlling the world, and part of his plan is an outright deception of Christians. We can easily understand that Satan is the father of lies and there is no truth in him. What is difficult to comprehend is that one out of three followers of cults were at one time believing Christians. If we know Satan is a liar, then why do so many Christians turn away from fundamental Christianity and turn to Satan's cults for spiritual answers? Because they were DECEIVED! They believed a lie and are now in bondage. God's

CONCLUSION

word wasn't branded on their hearts and His truths burning in their lives. They have *added* their theories to the Bible, which change the context of the Word of God entirely.

Satan wants a secularization of Christianity where Christians lack discernment and are no longer sensitive to the Holy Spirit. A slow regression from the truth so that a sensitivity to right and wrong is no longer understood. A hardening of the soul to spiritual truth. What will be accepted then is the worldly conception of love and wisdom which is shallow, lacking the deep, penetrating insight and power of the Holy Spirit. Then it will be difficult to distinguish the Christian from the non-Christian. This is the powerful spell and spiritual corruption of the anti-Christ, a gradual drawing away; desensitizing; eventual acceptance; rebellion; and then renunciation of the truth.

Paul wrote to Timothy telling him to *guard what has been trusted to your care. Turn away from godless chatter and the opposing ideas of what is falsely called knowledge which some have professed and in so doing have wandered from the faith* (I Timothy 6:20 NIV).

As we have seen within the last few years, beliefs in witchcraft and other occult religions have experienced a steady growth. We need, more than ever before, discernment within the body of Christ. Any new doctrines or theories which surface should be tested and weighed within the context of the Word of God. If a particular doctrine or belief does not adhere to scripture then we must discern the nature of that doctrine and *its origins.* If it doesn't come from God, it is not of God.

The temperaments do not glorify God. God is glorifed when Christians produce fruit—the Fruit of the Spirit. The character of God, or Christlikeness, is the Fruit of the Spirit. God is love and the Christian expresses love through the true divine nature of the Holy Spirit. *If we love one another, God dwelleth in us . . . Hereby know we that we dwell in him, and he in us, because he hath given us of his Spirit* (I John 5:12-13).

God hasn't revealed to mankind everything about our existence, but he did tell us what he wanted us to know. Many philosophers have tried to attain greater wisdom than the Creator in attempts to explain the mysteries of the universe. Mysteries which will never be revealed until we reach our heavenly home. If philosophers would seek to understand what God has revealed of Himself, they would discover the glorious majesty and power of Jehovah God. The one true God who rules everything in the heavens and earth with His righteousness and wisdom.

The temperaments, astrology, or any of the other numerous New Age personality systems may offer an ancient philosophical theory to understanding the complexities of the personality, but only the Savior, Jesus Christ can offer the faith, hope, peace, and eternal life to a lost personality.

When Christians are confronted and bombarded with New Age philosophies, we must turn to the truths found in the Bible. God's word reveals the truth for all of mankind, transforming the mind, enlightening the soul, and is the source of abundant, spiritual food for living now and life eternal. August H. Strong once expressed so well the relationship between God, man, and the Bible, "The Bible is a telescope between man and God; it is the rending of a veil."[3]

Historical References Of The Temperaments

A synopsis of Greek philosophy, the temperament theory, and astrology. This brief historical account includes only a small portion of the historical figures who taught and practiced the temperaments.

Babylon, Assyria, and Chaldea
Astrology
Witchcraft
Divination
The Pagan Gods

850 B.C.   **Homer Epics—***Iliad and Odyssey*
Doctrinal belief that anything which possesses strength or power is worshipped as a god.

600 B.C.   **The Cult of Asclepius**
Asclepius was worshipped as healing god and physician.

TEMPERAMYSTICISM

600 B.C.	**Thales of Miletus** Beginning of Greek philosophy. Doctrine that all things were filled with "gods." Water was divine source. All living things evolved from "fishes." Predicted eclipse of 585 B.C. by astrology.
610-546 B.C.	**Anaximander** Pupil of Thales. Universe is immortal and, therefore, divine. Expounded on Thales' theory. Believed god is a composite of all of nature—earth, water, fire, air, day, and night.
546-505 B.C.	**Anaximenes** Pupil of Anaximander. Believed "Air" was most divine containing all of the universe and the source for all things.
582-507 B.C.	**Pythagoras** of Samos Taught the doctrine of transmigration (immortality and reincarnation of the soul). Learned astrology from the Persians, Chaldeans, & Egyptians. ". . . worshipped knowledge and wisdom as the source of salvation."[1] "Fire" was the divine source of all life while lesser gods were planets, stars, sun, moon, earth, and the other elements. Applied mathematical principles to Greek astrology.
515-? B.C.	**Parmenides** of Elea, Italy Believed "thought" was divine. Only what one can visualize is real and divine.
580-488? B.C.	**Xenophanes** of Colophon Philosopher in Asia Minor.
521-487 B.C.	**Heraclitus** of Ephesus Doctrine of the microcosm & macrocosm. His philosophy of the divine elements (Earth, Air, Fire, and Water) influenced Empedocles. Believed "Fire" was the supreme deity. "The

HISTORICAL REFERENCES OF THE TEMPERAMENTS

	death of fire is birth for air, and the death of air is birth for water."[2]
500-428 B.C.	**Anaxagoras** of Klazomenai of Asia Minor Charged with blasphemy and exiled from Athens in the year 430 B.C. as a result of his denial of the planetary divinities.
470-399 B.C.	**Socrates** of Athens Philosopher. Believed self-knowledge and the soul were divinities.
483-423 B.C.	**Empedocles** of Acragas, Sicily Incorporated the four gods of the elements (Earth, Air, Fire, and Water) as separate and definable deities. Also, thought "Love" and "Strife" were divine forces which united or separated the elements. Pupil of Pythagoras. Announced he had achieved immortality and was now a "god."
460-377 B.C.	**Hippocrates** of Cos—Hippocratic School Incorporated Empedocles' conception of the four divine elements (or bodily humours; also known as the temperaments) into the function of human bodies. The elemental gods of nature ruled over the four bodily humours: sanguine, choleric, melancholy, and phlegmatic.
429-347 B.C.	**Plato** Studied Pythagoras doctrine of transmigration of the soul and Empedocles' conception of the world.
384-322 B.C.	**Aristotle** Defined the elemental gods into his principles of Earth (cold & dry), Water (cold & wet), Fire (hot & dry), and Air (hot & dry).
355-263 B.C.	**Zeno**, founder of Stoic school Influenced by Heraclitus.

280 B.C.	**Berosus** Established astrology school at Cos.	
1-33 A.D. (approximate)	**Birth and Earthly Life of Jesus Christ**	
54-68	**Nero,** Emperor to Rome Fire in Rome 64 A.D. Christians accused, persecuted, and martyred.	
129-199	**Galen**, Stoic physician & philosopher Expounded on temperament theory and used it with astrological medicine. Physician to the gladiators and Marcus Aurelius.	
121-180	**Marcus Aurelius** One of the first Roman emperors (161 A.D.) to begin the successive persecution of the Christians. Believed the soul at death was reabsorbed into the universe.	
218	**Heliogabalus**, "emperor of the sun." Sun worship at its peak. At 14 proclaimed himself universal god over every form of life, including the divine planets and elements. Was assassinated for his presumptions.	
400-1200	**Christianity slowly replaces Roman Paganism**	
354-430	**Saint Augustine** Accepted astrology, then later, he became strong opponent.	
1098-1179	**Saint Hildegard** of Bingen Wrote on the relationship between humours, temperaments, destiny, astrology, and astrological medicine.	
1115-1180	**John of Salisbury** Anti-astrology. Claimed astrological precepts were against free-will and God.	

HISTORICAL REFERENCES OF THE TEMPERAMENTS

1172-1235   **Michael Scott**
Wrote *Liber Introductorius*. Theologian and Astrologer to Frederick II.

1200-1280   **Saint Albertus Magnus**
Birth of Astronomy. Disassociated astrology from religious beliefs.

1225-1274   **Saint Thomas Aquinas**
At one time was advocate of astrology, later vehemently anti-astrology.

1384-1464   **Michael Savonarola** of Padua
Astrologer/physician. Combined temperaments and astrology with bodily functions & taught his beliefs that the aspects of the planets affected people.

1400?   **Galeotto Marzio Da Narnic**
Promiscuous Doctrine—On astrology and how the humours of the body were affected by the planets.

1400?   **John Lichtenberger**, German Astrologer.
Counseled Pope regarding astrological influences and advised him regarding certain diseases associated with the melancholy temperament and phlegm.

1497-1558   **Jean Francois Fernel** of Amiens
Professor of Medicine in Paris. Wrote on physiology, elements, humours, temperaments, and astrology.

1366-?   **Nicholas of Lynne**, Englishman
Lecturer at the University of Oxford. Interested in astrological medicine. Composed calendars between 1387-1462 of which several are preserved in English libraries. Calendars contained human anatomy and its relationship to the signs of the zodiac. Associated humours and temperaments with the planets. Was a priest of the Carmelite religion.

TEMPERAMYSTICISM

1452-1529	**Leonardo Da Vinci**	

Believed the earth was composed of the four elements of earth, air, fire, and water. All human souls descended to earth from the sun.

1493-1541 **Aureolus Theophrastus Paracelsus**
aka Bombast von Hohenheim
Condemned all medical teaching which was not based on experience. Anti-Galenic.

1523-1583 **Thomas (Liebler) Erastus**
Philosopher, theologian, and physician. Opposed astrology on scriptural grounds. Believed astrology was magic and totally opposed to Godly principles.

1537-? **Jacob Scholl**, Strasburg
Wrote "A Brief Application of Astrology to Medicine." This treatise contained information on the zodiac signs, planets, elemental humours, temperaments, astrological houses and their aspects in relation to disease.

1627-1691 **Robert Boyle**
Father of Chemistry. Against temperament and humoural theory.

Reference Bibliography

INTRODUCTION
1. Littauer, Florence, *After Every Wedding Comes A Marriage,* Oregon: Harvest House Publishers, 1981.

CHAPTER ONE
1. Drapela, Victor J., *A Review of Personality Theories,* Illinois: Charles C. Thomas Publisher, 1987, p. 591, requoted from Erich Fromm, 1947, p. 59.
2. Ibid, p. 591.
3. Littauer, Florence, *Personality Plus,* New Jersey: Fleming H. Revell Company, 1983, p. 16.
4. Ibid, p. 17.

CHAPTER TWO
1. Von Humboldt, Friedrich Heinrich Alexander, quoted from *The Encyclopedia of Religious Quotations,* Edited & Compiled by Frank S. Mead, Westwood, New Jersey: Fleming H. Revell Company, 1965, p. 85.

CHAPTER THREE
1. Kerenyi, C., *Asklepios, Archetypal Image of the Physician's Existence,* Bollingen Series, LXV.3, New York: Pantheon Books, 1959, p. 61, reprinted from "Decorum," Ed. and tr. Jones, II, 286f.
2. Ibid, p. 7.
3. Sigerist, Henry E., *A History of Medicine,* Volume II: Early Greek, Hindu, and Persian Medicine, New York: Oxford University Press, 1961, p. 20.

4. Ibid, pp. 21-22.
5. Edelstein, Ludwig, *Ancient Medicine*, Maryland: The Johns Hopkins Press, 1967, p. 372.
6. Sigerist, p. 51.
7. Edelstein, pp. 239, 372.
8. Kerenyi, p. 11.
9. Sigerist, p. 45.
10. Ibid, p. 61.
11. Ibid, p. 45.
12. Edelstein, Vol. II, p. 179.
13. Ibid, p. 134.
14. Edelstein, Vol. I, p. 49, requoted from Justinus, Dialogues, 69, 3.
15. Edelstein, Vol. I, p. 419.

CHAPTER FOUR

1 Thorndike, Lynn, *History of Magic & Experimental Science*, Vol. III, New York: The Macmillan Company, 1923, p. 411.
2. Lund, Fred, *Greek Medicine*, Paul B. Hoeber, New York: Medical Book Department of Harper & Bros., 1936
3. Edelstein, Vol. I, p. 215.
4. Ibid, p. 214.
5. Ibid, p. 240.
6. Rawson, Hugh & Miller, Margaret, *The New International Dictionary of Quotations, Hippocrates Aphorisms,* New York: E. P. Dutton, 1986, p. 288.
7. Graubard, Mark, *Astrology and Alchemy: Two Fossil Sciences,* New York: University of Minnesota, Philosophical Library, 1953, p. 255.
8. Wright, M.R., *Empedocles the Extant Fragment,* New Haven and London: Yale University Press, 1981, pp. 26-27, 314.
9. Millerd, Clara Elizabeth, *On The Interpretation of Empedocles,* New York: Garland Pub., Inc., 1980, p. 47.
10. Lambridis, Helle, *Empedocles,* Alabama: The University of Alabama Press, 1976, p. 19, requoted from Empedocles' *Purifications* (DK, 31B fr. 112).
11. Ibid, p. 45 (DK, 31B fr. 17, 1.34-35).

12. Ibid, p. 141 (DK, 31B fr. 57).
13. Ibid, p. 119 (DK, 31B fr. 117).
14. Ibid, p. 130 (DK, 31B fr. 146).

CHAPTER FIVE

1. *The Meditations of Marcus Aurelius,* Translated by George Long, The Harvard Classics, Vol. 2, edited by Charles W. Eliot, LL.D., New York: P.F. Collier & Son Corp, 1937, p. 192.
2. Ibid, p. 314.
3. Ibid, p. 314.
4. Ibid, pp. 215-216.

CHAPTER SIX

1. Cohu, J. R., *The Bible and Modern Thought,* V, Reprinted in The Encyclopedia of Religious Quotations, Edited & Compiled by Frank S. Mead, MCMLXV, Westwood, New Jersey: Fleming H. Revell Company, p. 25.
2. Festugiere, Andre-Jean, O. P., *Personal Religion Among the Greeks,* Berkeley & Los Angeles: University of California Press, 1954, p. 51.
3. Thorndike, Vol. V, p. 117.
4. Hall, Manly Palmer, *The Story of Astrology,* Washington Square, Philadelphia: David McKay Company, 1943, p. 12.
5. Walzer, R., *Galen on Jews and Christians,* London: Oxford University Press, Geoffrey Cumberlege, 1949, p. 24.
6. Ibid, p. 24.
7. Ibid, p. 24.
8. Ibid, p. 25.
9. Ibid, p. 25.
10. Ibid, p. 24.
11. Ibid, p. 76.
12. Ibid, p. 25.
13. Zusne, Leonard, *Biographical Dictionary of Psychology,* Westport, Connecticut: Greenwood Press, pp. 147-148.
14. Ibid, p. 147-148.
15. May, Margaret Tallmadge, *Galen On the Usefulness of the Parts of the Body,* Translated from the Greek, New York: Cornell University Press, 1968, p. 730.

16. Thorndike, Vol. II, p. 134.
17. Ibid, p. 151.
18. Ibid, p. 152.
19. Ibid, p. 151.
20. Hallesby, O., *Temperament and the Christian Faith*, 1962, Minnesota: Augsburg Publishing House, 1962, p. 11.
21. Ibid, pp. 105-106.

CHAPTER SEVEN
1. Thorndike, Vol. III, p. 364.
2. Ibid, p. 364.
3. Ibid, p. 363.
4. Thorndike, Vol. V, p. 475.
5. Thorndike, Vol. II, pp. 56-57.
6. Ibid, p. 344.
7. Stillman, John Maxson, *Theophrastus Bombastus Von Hohenheim, called Paracelsus*, Chicago: The Open Court Pub. Company, 1920, p. 48.
8. Thorndike, Vol. II, p. 344.

CHAPTER EIGHT
1. Longfellow, Henry Wadsworth, quoted from *The Encyclopedia of Religious Quotations*, Edited & Compiled by Frank S. Mead, Westwood, New Jersey: Fleming H. Revell Company, 1965, p. 418.
2. Kirk, G. S., Raven, J. E., Schofield, M., *The Prehistoric Philosophers*, Second Edition, Cambridge, New York: Cambridge University Press, 1957, 1983, p. 59.
3. Rose, H. J., *Religion in Greece and Rome*, New York: Harper and Row, p. 127.

CHAPTER NINE
1. Harre, Rom & Lamb, Roger, *Encyclopedic Dictionary of Psychology*, Vol. 3, Edited by Raymond J. Corsini, p. 493.
2. Bobgan, Martin and Deidre, *Psycho Heresy*, Santa Barbara, California: East Gate Publishers, 1987, p. 24.
3. Harre, Vol. 3, p. 410.

4. Carbonell, Mels and Rohm, Robert, *Personality Profile,* Georgia: In Touch Ministries, 1990.

CHAPTER TEN

1. Marrs, Texe, *Mystery Mark of the New Age,* Westchester, Illinois: Crossway Books, 1988, p. 87.
2. Cumont, Franz, *Astrology and Religion Among the Greeks and Romans,* New York and London: G.P. Putnam's Sons, The Knickerbocker Press, 1912, p. 31.
3. Saint Augustine, *On Christian Doctrine,* translated by J. F. Shaw, Encyclopedia Britannica, Inc., p. 647.
4. Thorndike, Vol. II, pp. 13-14.
5. Cumont, p. 4.
6. Culver, Roger B. & Ianna, Phillip A., *Astrology True or False,* A Scientific Evalutation, Promethius Books, 1988, p. 2, quote reprinted from Bok, B. J., Physics Today, January, 1977, p. 84.

CHAPTER ELEVEN

1. Culver, Roger B. & Ianna, Philip A., *Astrology True or False?* A Scientific Evaluation, Prometheus Books, 1988, p. 2, quote reprinted from Bok, B.J., Physics Today, January 1977, p. 201.
2. Corsini, Raymond J., & Ozaki, Bonnie D., *Encyclopedia of Psychology,* New York: Wiley Pub. Company, 1984, p. 24.
3. Strong, Augustus H., *American Poets & Their Theology,* 11, 2; Judson Press, *The Encyclopedia of Religious Quotations,* Frank S. Mead, Westwood, New Jersey: Fleming H. Revell Company, p. 33.

HISTORICAL REFERENCES

1. Hack, Roy Kenneth, Litt. (OXON), *God in Greek Philosophy to the Time of Socrates,* Princeton: Princeton University Press, 1931, p. 47.
2. Kahn, Charles H., *Anaximander and the Origins of Greek Cosmology,* New York and London: Columbia University Press, 1960, p. 184.

General Bibliography

Acherknecht, Erwin H., *A Short History of Medicine,* New York: Ronald Press Company, 1968.

Allbutt, T. Clifford, *Greek Medicine in Rome,* Benjamin Blom, Inc., 1970.

Angus, Samuel, *The Mystery-Religions: A Study in the Religious Background of Early Christianity,* New York, New York: Dover Publications, 1975.

Boyce, Benjamin, *The Theophrastan Character,* In England to 1642, New York: The Humanities Press, 1967.

Burnet, John, *Platonism,* Berkeley, California: University of California Press, 1928.

Burnet, John, *Early Greek Philosophy,* Fourth Edition, London: Adam & Charles Black, 1930.

Burnet, John, *Greek Philosophy,* Part I, St. Martins Street, London: Macmillan & Company, Limited, 1914.

Carbonell, Mels and Rohm, Robert, *Personality Profile,* In Touch Ministries, Georgia, 1990.

Cornford, Francis MacDonald, *Before and After Socrates,* Cambridge at the University Press, 1962.

Cornford, F. M., *From Religion to Philosophy,* New York, Harper & Row, 1957.

Cornford, F. M., *Greek Religious Thought from Homer to the Age of Alexander,* New York: AMS Press, 1969.

Cleve, Felix M., *The Philosophy of Anaxagoras,* The Hague, Netherlands: Martinus Nijhoff, 1973.

Crabb, Larry, *Inside Out,* Colorado: Navpress, 1988.

Cumont, Franz, *Astrology and Religion Among the Greeks and Romans,* New York, New York: Dover Publications, 1960.

Cumont, Franz, *The Oriental Religions in Roman Paganism,* Chicago: The Open Court Publishing Company, 1911.

Cumont, Franz, *After Life in Roman Paganism,* New York, New York: Dover Publications, 1959.

Cumont, Franz, *Mysteries of Mithra,* New York, New York: Dover Publications, Inc., 1956.

DeParrie, Paul and Pride, Mary, *Unholy Sacrifices of The New Age,* Illinois: Crossway Books, 1978.

Dubos, Rene, *Mirage of Health,* Anchor Books, Doubleday & Company, Inc., 1959.

Edelstein, E. J. and L., *Asclepius,* Baltimore, 1945.

Elliott, James, Sir, *Outlines of Greek and Roman Medicine,* Milford House, 1971.

Empedocles, *Empedocles, the Extant Fragments,* Yale University Press, 1981.

Encyclopedia of World Mythology, New York: Galahad Books, a division of A & W Promotional Book Corp., 1975.

Eysenck, H. J. and Nias, D. K. B., *Astrology Science or Superstition?* New York: St. Martin's Press, 1982.

Festugiere, Andre-Jean, *Personal Religion Among the Greeks,* Berkeley and Los Angeles, California: University of California Press, 1954.

Fowler, W. Warde, *The Religious Experience of the Roman People,* New York: Cooper Square Publishers, Inc., 1971.

Furley, David J., and Allen, R. E., *Studies in Presoteric Philosophy,* Vol. I, New York: Humanities Press, 1970.

Galen, *Galen on the Natural Faculties,* William Heimeman, G. P. Putnam's Sons, 1916.

Galen, *Galen on the Usefulness of the Parts of the Body,* Cornell University Press, 1968.

Goldberg, Herbert S., *Hippocrates, Father of Medicine,* New York: Franklin Watts, Inc., 1963.

Grant, Michael, *Roman Myths,* New York: Charles Scribner's Sons, 1971.

Green, Robert Montraville, *A Translation of Galen's Hygiene,* Illinois: Charles C. Thomas Publisher, 1951.

BIBLIOGRAPHY

Guthrie, W. K. C., *The Greek Philosophers,* New York: Harper & Row, 1960.

Haggard, Howard Wilcox, *Mystery, Magic and Medicine; The Rise of Medicine from Superstition to Science,* Doubleday, Doran, 1933.

Hallesby, O., *Temperament and the Christian Faith,* Minneapolis, Minneasota: Augsburg Publishing House, 1962.

Hippocrates, *Hippocrates,* Harvard University Press, 1959-1962.

Jaeger, Werner Wilhelm, *The Theology of the Early Greek Philosophers,* Clarendon Press, 1964.

Jayne, Walter Addison, *The Healing Gods of Ancient Civilizations,* University Books, 1962.

Kahn, Charles H., *The Art and Thought of Heraclitus,* An Edition of the fragments with translation and commentary, Massachusetts: Cambridge University Press, 1979.

Keefe, Robert and Janica A., *Walter Pater and the Gods of Disorder,* Athens, Ohio: Ohio University Press, 1988.

Kirk, G. S., Raven, J. E., Schofield, M., *The Presocratic Philosophers,* Second Edition, Cambridge, New York: Cambridge University Press, 1957, 1983.

Kirk, G. S., *The Nature of Greek Myths,* Woodstock, New York: The Overlook Press, 1975.

LaHaye, Tim, *Why You Act the Way You Do,* Third Edition, Wheaton, Illinois: Living Books, Tyndale House Publishers, Inc., 1984.

LaHaye, Tim, *Your Temperament Can Be Changed,* Twelfth Edition, Wheaton, Illinois: Tyndale House Publishers, Inc., 1987.

LaHaye, Tim, *Spirit-Controlled Temperament,* 720 Fifth Avenue, New York, New York, 10019: Phoenix Press, Walker and Company, 1986.

LaHaye, Tim, *Spirit-Controlled Temperament,* Living Studies, Illinois: Tyndale House Publishers, Inc., 1966.

LaHaye, Tim, *Transformed Temperaments,* Wheaton, Illinois: Tyndale House Publishers, 1971.

Lawton, W. C., *The Successors of Homer,* New York: The Macmillan Company, 1898.

Levine, Edwin Burton, *Hippocrates,* New York: Twayne Publishers, Inc., 1971.

Lincoln, Bruce, *Myth Cosmos and Society*, Cambridge: Harvard University Press, 1986.

Littauer, Florence, *After Every Wedding Comes A Marriage*, Oregon: Harvest House Publishers, 1981.

Littauer, Florence, *How to Get Along With Difficult People*, Oregon: Harvest House Publishers, 1984.

Littauer, Florence, *Personalities in Power, The Making of Great Leaders*, Louisiana: Huntington House, Inc., 70505.

Littauer, Florence, *Personality Plus: How to Understand Others by Understanding Yourself*, New Jersey: Fleming H. Revell Company, 1983.

Littauer, Florence, *Your Personality Tree*, Texas: Word Publishers, 1986.

Mircea Eliade, Editor in Chief, *The Encyclopedia of Religion*, Vol. 1, New York: Macmillan Publishing Company, 1987.

Palmer, Robert E. A., *Roman Religion and Roman Empire*, Five Essays, Philadelphia, Pennsylvania: University of Pennsylvania Press, 1974.

Palmer, Helen, *The Enneagram: Understanding Yourself and the Others in Your Life*, San Francisco: Harper & Row Publishers, 1988.

Perowne, Stewart, *Roman Mythology*, USA:The Hamlyn Publishing Group, 1969.

Riso, Don Richard, *Personality Types Using the Enneagram for Self-Discovery*, Boston: Houghton Mifflin Company, 1987.

Stadelman, Luis J., *The Hebrew Conception of the World*, Rome, Italy: Pontifical Biblical Institute, 1970.

Taylor, Lily Ross, *The Cults of Ostia*, Chicago: Ares Publishers, Inc., 1976.

Thorndike, Lynn, *A History of Magic and Experimental Science*, Columbia University Press, 1923.

Thorwald, Jurgen, *Science and Secrets of Early Medicine; Egypt, Mesopotamia, India, China, Mexico, Peru*, Harcourt, Brace & World, 1962.

Toynbee, Arnold J., *Greek Historical Thought*, New York: J. M. Dent & Sons Ltd., MCMXXIV.

Veyne, Paul, *Did the Greeks Believe in Their Myths?* Chicago: University of Chicago Press, 1988.

BIBLIOGRAPHY

Walzer, R., *Galen on Jews and Christians,* London: Oxfcrd University Press, Geoffrey Cumberlege, 1969.

Whyte, Alexander, *Treasury of Alexander Whyte,* Baker Publishers.

Zeller, Eduard, *Outlines of the History of Greek Philosophy,* Routledge & Kegan Paul, 1963.

Books & Tapes by Starburst Publishers

Like A Bulging Wall   —Robert Borrud

Will you survive the 1990's economic crash? This book shows how debt, greed, and covetousness, along with a lifestyle beyond our means, has brought about an explosive situation in this country. Gives "call" from God to prepare for judgement in America, Also Lists TOP-RATED U.S. BANKS and SAVINGS & LOANS.

                            (trade paper)   ISBN 0914984284   **$8.95**

Teenage Mutant Ninja Turtles Exposed!   —Joan Hake Robie

Looks closely at the national popularity of *Teenage Mutant Ninja Turtles*. Tells what they teach and how this "turtle" philosophy affects children (and adults) mentally, emotionally, socially, morally, and spiritually. The book gives the answer to what we can do about the problem.

                            (trade paper)   ISBN 0914984314   **$5.95**

What To Do When The Bill Collector Calls!
Know Your Rights   —David L. Kelcher, Jr.

Reveals the unfair debt collection practices that some agencies use and how this has led to the invasion of privacy, bankruptcy, marital instability, and the loss of jobs. The reader is told what he can do about the problem.

                            (trade paper)   ISBN 0914984322   **$9.95**

The Quick Job Hunt Guide   —Robert D. Siedle

Gives techniques to use when looking for a job. Networking, Following the Ten-Day Plan, and Avoiding the Personnel Department, are some of the ways to "land that job!"

                            (trade paper)   ISBN 0914984330   **$7.95**

Turmoil In The Toy Box II   —Joan Hake Robie

This book takes a hard look at the popular "Nintendo" games, the "Batman" craze, "Ghostbusters," "Freddy" from *A Nightmare on Elm Street,* Dungeons and Dragons and much more. Seeks to make every parent aware of the potential for mental, emotional and spiritual harm from allowing their children access to toys and TV that will give them more of a foundation in the occult than in God's teaching.

                            (trade paper)   ISBN 0914984209   **$8.95**

Turmoil In The Toy Box II—audio   —Joan Hake Robie

Narrated by Joan Hake Robie, author of the book *Turmoil In The Toy Box II,* this 60 minute audio explains how many parents don't realize the role that toys and cartoons play in their child's life. It reveals some of the hidden and not so hidden messages directed to the minds of our children.

                   (audio cassette tape)   ISBN 0914984268   **$7.95**

Books & Tapes by Starburst Publishers—cont'd.

The Truth About Dungeons And Dragons—audio
—Joan Hake Robie

Explains the game of Dungeons and Dragons and lists the bizarre cast of characters which includes demons, dragons, witches, zombies, harpies, gnomes and creatures who cast spells and exercise supernatural powers. It tells how Dungeons and Dragons dabbles in the occult, encourages sex and violence and is a form of Devil worship.

(audio cassette tape) 091498425X **$7.95**

Courting The King Of Terrors
—Frank Carl
with Joan Hake Robie

Why are so many people turning to Mental, Spiritual and Physical suicide? This book probes the relentless ills that are destroying the American family, and offers counsel to families in crisis. "I know about suicide," says Frank Carl. "I lost a Brother and a Sister to that monster!"

(trade paper) ISBN 0914984187 **$7.95**

Horror And Violence—The Deadly Duo In The Media
—Phil Phillips
and Joan Hake Robie

Americans are hooked on violence! Muggings, kindappings, rape and murders are commonplace via your TV set. This book not only brings you up to date on what is happening in the media in general, but also will help you and your children survive with integrity in a complex media environment.

(trade paper) ISBN 0914984160 **$8.95**

Halloween And Satanism
—Phil Phillips
and Joan Hake Robie

This book traces the origins of Halloween and gives the true meaning behind this celebration of "fun and games." Jack-O-Lanterns, Cats, Bats, and Ghosts are much more than costumes and window decorations. In this book you will discover that involvement in any form of the occult will bring you more than "good fortune." It will lead you deeper and deeper into the Satanic realm, which ultimately leads to death.

(trade paper) ISBN 091498411X **$8.95**

Turmoil In The Toy Box
—Phil Phillips

A shocking expose of the toy and cartoon industry—unmasks the New Age, Occult, Violent, and Satanic influences that have invaded the once innocent toy box. Over 150,000 in print.

(trade paper) ISBN 0914984047 **$8.95**

The Rock Report — Fletcher A. Brothers

An "uncensored" look into today's Rock Music scene—provides the reader with the necessary information and illustrations to make intelligent decisions about rock music and its influence on the mind.

(trade paper) ISBN 0914984136 **$6.95**

The Quest For Truth — Ken Johnson

A "Pilgrim's Progress" type book that is designed to lead the reader to a realization that there is no solution to the world's problems, nor is there a purpose to life, apart from Jesus Christ. (A unique allegorical expose of truth.)

(trade paper) ISBN 0914984217 **$7.95**

Man And Wife For Life — Joseph Kanzlemar, Ed.D.

A penetrating and often humorous look into real life situations of married people. Helps the reader get a new understanding of the problems and relationships within marriage.

(trade paper) ISBN 0914984233 **$7.95**

A Candle In Darkness (novel) — June Livesay

A heartwarming novel (based on fact), set in the mountains of Ecuador. This book is filled with love, suspense, and intrigue. The first in a series of books by June Livesay.

(trade paper) ISBN 0914984225 **$8.95**

Alzheimer's—Does "The System Care?"
— Ted Valenti, M.S.W. & Paula Valenti, R.N.

Experts consider Alzheimer's disease to be the "the disease of the century." More than half the one million elderly people residing in American nursing homes have "senile dementia." This book reveals a unique observation as to the cause of Alzheimers's and the care of its victims.

(hard cover) ISBN 0914984179 **$14.95**

The Great Pretender — Rose Hall Warnke
with Joan Hake Robie

An amusing, revealing, and oftimes shocking look into the life and ministry of Mike and Rose Warnke.

(trade paper) ISBN 0914984039 **$8.95**

The Subtle Snare — Joan Hake Robie

You read about the PTL Scandal . . . Now read about the solution. This book will cause you to examine your own life so that you may avoid *The Subtle Snare*

(trade paper) ISBN 0914984128 **$8.95**

Books & Tapes by Starburst Publishers—cont'd.

Inch by Inch . . . Is It a Cinch?   —Phyllis Miller
Is it a cinch to lose weight? If your answer is "NO," you must read this book. Read about the intimate details of one woman's struggle for love and acceptance.
(trade paper)   ISBN 0914984152 $8.95

Devotion in Motion   —Joan Hake Robie
Worship in a new dimension! Leads the reader into a deeper, more creative experience of worship.
(trade paper)   ISBN 0914984004 $4.95

You Can Live In Divine Health   —Joyce Boisseau
Medical and Spiritual considerations concerning the dilemma of sickness. "Does the Christian have an inherited right to divine health?"
(trade paper)   ISBN 0914984020 $6.95

To My Jewish Friends With Love   —Christine Hyle
"One of the finest Jewish evangelism tools I have ever seen," writes Dr. Charles R. Taylor of TODAY IN BIBLE PROPHECY. Just slip this book into the hands of your Jewish friends and say, "I LOVE YOU."
(booklet)   0006028098 $1.00

Purchasing Information

Most listed books and tapes are available from your favorite Bookstore, either from current stock or special order. You may also order direct from STARBURST PUBLISHERS. When ordering enclose full payment plus $2.00* for shipping and handling ($2.50* if Canada or Overseas). Payment in US Funds only. Please allow two to three weeks minimum (longer overseas) for delivery. Make checks payable to and mail to STARBURST PUBLISHERS, P.O. Box 4123, LANCASTER, PA 17604. Prices subject to change without notice. Catalog available upon request.

* We reserve the right to ship your order the least expensive way. If you desire first class (domestic) or air shipment (overseas) please enclose shipping funds as follows: First Class within the USA enclose $4.00, Airmail Canada enclose $5.00, and Overseas enclose 30% (minimum $5.00) of total order. All remittance must be in US Funds.